TOOLS
FOR
LEADERS

Indispensable
Graphic Organizers, Protocols,
and Planning Guidelines for Working
and Learning Together

MARJORIE LARNER

■SCHOLASTIC

New York • Toronto • London • Auckland • Sydney
Mexico City • New Delhi • Hong Kong • Buenos Aires

Cover design: Jorge J. Namerow
Interior design: LDL Designs
Acquiring Editor: Lois Bridges
Editor: Gloria Pipkin
Production Editor: Amy Gilbert
Copy Editor: Chris Borris

ISBN-13: 978-0-439-02427-3
ISBN-10: 0-439-02427-7
Copyright © 2007 by Marjorie Larner
All rights reserved. Published by Scholastic Inc.
Printed in the U.S.A.
1 2 3 4 5 6 7 8 9 10   40   12 11 10 09 08 07

To Patricia Fitzgerald Carini

"Still here, still acting on the legacy of those ideas . . ."

CONTENTS

ACKNOWLEDGMENTS

When I first imagined this book, I looked forward to writing the acknowledgments and naming everyone who has in one way or another contributed. Now that I am finally at the point of writing it down, it is overwhelming to try to capture the depth of honor and gratitude I feel for the sincere dedication of my colleagues, their brilliant students, and the support of my family and friends.

Colorado Critical Friends Group Facilitators, my true home base, includes the most dedicated kindred spirits I could ever wish for. Theress Pidick, Stevi Quate, and Dave Schmid provide partnership that sustains and challenges me every day.

National School Reform Faculty staff and colleagues, with unending generosity and integrity to the mission, are a source of deep strength, wisdom, and knowledge.

Others I want to thank and honor include the following:

The Public Education and Business Coalition, Boulder Valley School District, BVSD Elementary Principals Group, and the Collaborative Inquiry Cohort, for opportunities to create and grow.

Joy Hood, Anne Goudvis, Carrie Symons, and Catherine Rubin, for ongoing feedback and problem solving in work and in life.

Administrators and friends Scott Winston, Tom Kasper, Kathy Hatz, Sammye Wheeler, Stephanie Torrez, and Libby Klingsmith, for opportunities to cocreate.

Colorado schools where this work was developed with teachers, including Casey Middle School, Prairie Middle School, Thunder Mountain Elementary School, Creekside Elementary, Hunters Glen Elementary, and Dakota Valley Elementary.

Everyone at Aspen Creek K–8 for year after year of pushing the boundaries of what we can learn together about teaching and learning.

Colleagues and teachers whose lessons I continue to carry: Deborah Meier, Stephanie Harvey, Karolynne Gee, Ellin Keene, Susan McIver, Chryse Hutchins, Cris Tovani, Susan Gold, Sam Bennett, Laura Jordan, Jean Houston, Peg Rubin, Val Wheeler, Rachael Kessler, Laura Weaver, and Sarah Labounty.

For their patience and belief, my friends: Janice Wall, Sandy Stollery, Karen Burke, Erny Walker, Marthe Gold, Sandra Kennedy, Sue Pisano, Theron Labounty, Beth Record, Susan Gitt, and Faryl Palles.

I had the guidance of three amazing editors through the course of writing this book: Danny Miller, valued friend as well as great writer and editor, whose ideas and heart are embedded in the fiber of this book;

Gloria Pipkin, with the eye of an eagle, and gifts of insight about every aspect of writing; and

Lois Bridges, who had both a keen sense for what was needed and great sensitivity to what I wanted to accomplish.

The production team, particularly Amy Gilbert, Ray Coutu, Lauren Leon, and Chris Borris earned my deepest thanks and awe in taking on the challenge of turning the manuscript into a book.

Everything starts with my family's love and support:

my sister Judith Lowry for the courage to persevere and care deeply;

my brother Bernard Larner for his astute perceptions, which provide a backdrop to my view of the world;

their families and my extended family of cousins, who remind me what people can feel and be for one another;

Rosie Lee Jackson, who shares wisdom that whatever we do, we can be strong and loving;

finally, my three sons, Cass, Josh, and Alex Epstein, for the music of all kinds they bring to my life and the joy of watching them, now old enough to have their own dreams of helping the world, for all we've been through together, for keeping me determined, and for always making sure I keep wondering and learning.

FOREWORD

Over the last two decades we have experienced a sea change in the nature of ongoing professional learning by practicing teachers. For too long we endured "in-service training" that often consisted of discrete components disconnected from the needs of students and the realities of classroom teaching. "Professional development" has a more respectful ring to it, but too often it was little more than window dressing for the essentially passive nature of the enterprise. Rather than making us agents and active participants in our own professional growth, professional development was something delivered to us by outside experts.

Now, in the twenty-first century, teacher leaders have moved to the forefront and practitioners have become active participants in professional learning communities characterized by reflective practice, collaboration, and shared leadership. Guided by colleagues who are skilled facilitative leaders using proven structures and practices, teachers are shaping and experiencing the high-quality learning and sustained support they need to succeed.

One of those teacher leaders is Marjorie Larner, the author of the book you hold in your hands. *Tools for Leaders* draws on Marjorie's many years as an administrator and facilitator of collaborative work in schools. I first met Marjorie at the Denver-based Public Education and Business Coalition, where we worked together as staff developers along with some quite extraordinary educators. Every Monday we gathered around the conference room table and spent hours in spirited discourse about progressive educational practice and philosophy. It didn't take long to notice what Marjorie brought to that table. Her thoughtful and salient reflections always nudged the conversation further. How lucky we are that she has written a second book!

In *Tools for Leaders* she shares the resources and understanding developed in the field to support instructional coaches, administrators, and teacher leaders as they guide and facilitate groups, teams, and whole faculties to better serve every student by assuming ongoing control over their own learning needs.

Marjorie takes us step by step through the process of establishing effective professional learning communities, from setting the tone for shared ownership and responsibility to building a new culture of learning that values all perspectives—including those of students. Through formal structures and strategies known as protocols and a wealth of other tools, she equips us to manage complex change as well as to address resistance to it. You'll find the practical advice you need to manage logistics as well as the sophisticated under-standings and skill required to provide a safe environment for making our work public. In the end you'll succeed in turning standards into student learning.

— Stephanie Harvey

INTRODUCTION

*There is one thing stronger than all the armies of the world and that is
an idea whose time has come.*
—Victor Hugo

"If he gets twenty minutes one-on-one at the beginning of the day, he focuses and does great work. Otherwise it is a disaster from beginning to end." This lament from a teacher was the first note of my coaching day. We had been watching a new boy who had come into her class and refused to read or write. Finally, she had landed on something that helped him. Yet how could she implement this solution? "There is no way I can find twenty minutes first thing every day to devote to him, with twenty-five other kids in the room—who are, by the way, affected and influenced by him." With only a few minutes before the start of school, we had to talk about her students' responses to the new literacy program. But we were distracted and troubled over how to provide what this one bright young boy needed. What could she do? As a coach, what could I do?

If you face challenges such as this in working with teachers to meet the educational needs of every child, this book is for you. I write for all of you who take a leadership role in helping teachers in a school. Whether your job title identifies this as your major responsibility (for example, if you are a coach), or you are a principal or teacher with professional development as an aspect of your job, you will find tools in this book to help you facilitate and guide learning that gets to the heart of the work you do in your school.

While doing this work in the role of coach or instructional leader, you probably work in a lot of different ways in the course of even one day. You might already be facilitating discussions and coordinating in-service days. You might observe and provide feedback, plan with teachers or offer demonstration lessons, suggest readings and strategies in response to their questions. In building trust and relationships, I would guess that you have found at least a few kindred spirits who are always happy to work with you, though with others you have yet to find an entry point.

You know you are expected to help turn the school around or demonstrate progress by some discernable measure. Perhaps the focus is on higher test scores or district assessments, on new instructional strategies or programs, on an achievement gap, graduation rates, or other issues of equity.

Undoubtedly, you have times when you see you have made significant progress and times when you build on success. Yet, like me at times, you might sometimes worry that your work is only a drop in the bucket. There is still pressure for change to happen faster, to impact more classrooms, to increase every student's learning and achievement.

What Can You Do?

Using smart tools and thoughtful protocols to bring value and meet your purposes, to ensure teacher ownership and buy-in, to share expertise and new knowledge, professional development can be grounded in the reality and practice of the classroom. Rather than being the sole source of professional learning and growth, you can be the facilitator for a learning community, providing guidance, structure, and support as teachers establish habits for working and learning together that become the norm for school operations. You can be a resource for grade-level and department meetings, study groups, and other school-based collaborative endeavors in your school.

Imagine teachers entering the room for your beginning-of-the-year meeting. What is on their minds and what do they expect? Are they hopeful that the time will be spent on something relevant, but uncertain of how realistic everyone will be? Are they worrying about finding time to plan tomorrow's math lesson or getting home to make dinner for the family? Is anyone expecting a focus on something that will make a difference for students the next day?

Let's imagine, from a teacher's point of view, two different scenarios for the beginning of a meeting. In one, an administrator and an instructional coach stand in front of the group and tell you what you will be doing. They present information about a new writing-through-the-curriculum program you will be implementing in your classrooms. You are distracted by two teachers in the back of the room, whispering to each other. You wish you knew what they were saying. Every now and then you are given a few minutes to turn and talk to a partner about what you've heard, and then you listen to more information that you might find interesting and potentially helpful, if also somewhat overwhelming.

Your principal offers you a sign-up sheet for the coach to observe your efforts with this new program and offer feedback to support you with implementation. By the end of the meeting, you know you have to make some big changes, and you have questions about exactly how and what that will be. And you still have the first week's lessons to plan.

In another scenario, an administrator and coach open the meeting with a brief description of the new writing-through-the-curriculum program, the changes that will result, the needs they and the district hope it will address, and the potential challenges it poses. They ask each of you to think about what would help you implement this program in your classroom in a way that would benefit both you and your students. After a couple of minutes during which everyone has a chance to think, you break into smaller groups and each person gets a chance to reply.

You watch the responses to what others say. When a colleague says quietly, "I'm here because I was told to come and I'll just do what I have to," you see a few others laugh in commiseration. You think it might be okay to admit that you wish you'd get something to use the next day. After a quiet new teacher in her first year says she is drowning already and doesn't even know what to ask for, a third-year teacher says she hopes you can help one another during common planning time. Around the room, your colleagues express hopes and concerns, willingness and resistance.

You move into grade-level teams with the task of looking at the program materials, with a set of questions to guide your discussion. By the end of the short meeting, you have had a chance to listen and talk in small teams about what each person is already doing in his or her classroom, read about the new program, and consider how the two complement or work against each other to help your students. The whole group generates and records ideas to support application and to find time to work with one another on implementation in each classroom.

The principal, the coach, and two teachers promise to meet the next day to look through these ideas, send everyone a proposed plan via e-mail, and finalize it at the next week's faculty meeting. You leave with some trepidation about what is to come, though you are reassured that you will have company to share the challenge and the success with. You leave the room talking with a colleague about your plans for the first week.

How do these two meetings and plans compare? They both offer information and expectations for implementation of a new program. They both promise follow-up support. In the first meeting, individual teachers are invited to figure out how to implement a new program in their classrooms, with at least one coaching session. You might say there is trust in the autonomy of each teacher to determine what will work for her in her classroom. In the second scenario, the faculty is encouraged to work and learn together to share knowledge, values, and past experiences to help one another meet a new challenge, with the promise of a plan arising from their ideas.

Either of these approaches might yield results, though the results for each will differ in scope, benefit, and challenge. Individuals working alone are free to try out their best ideas without spending time in meetings or working toward consensus. They will not be held back trying to help someone else or stifle a great idea that works for them but not the group. A few great teachers can emerge from the pack and serve as mentors, as well as take on more challenging students. In these schools, you can find pockets of excellence.

Several individuals combining their ideas, experiences, knowledge, and support will generate many more ideas and possibilities. Small groups can build trust and embrace more voices. Inclusive groups make it possible for the whole school to hear the same message and establish consistent language and practice. You can push yourselves to overcome obstacles that have stood in the way of reaching every child and advocate for what is best for students in your school. In these schools you find consistent language and instructional approaches and a whole community striving toward excellence for every student.

No Longer Skimming the Surface

Some say that the time for individual and privatized classroom practice has passed. With a commitment to not miss even one child, we can no longer do it on our own. It is not a matter of choosing our preference for what is comfortable but rather an imperative to join together, learn from one another with our different backgrounds and expertise, and lend each other strength to push beyond our current capacities, for the sake of all students.

Just as you use thoughtfully developed tools in your classroom to manage and facilitate learning with a diverse group of young people, you can rely on artful tools to help you manage and facilitate a community of adult learners so your work together is productive and efficient and you achieve the ultimate goal—success for children in the classroom and beyond.

What Really Matters

There is a sense of urgency for all, no matter their race, native language, or disposition, to be engaged in the best of what our public school system can offer. It is more than one teacher can do alone. It takes multiple perspectives, multiple ideas, and diverse ways of seeing and thinking. It means providing unity, repetition, and consistency for students through their days and years in school. It requires time and support for teachers to build honest relationships, explore what they already know, discover new ideas, and see results through application.

At the heart of this approach to working and learning together is the basic human inclination toward relationship and connection. From this perspective, three foundational beliefs form the basis for the organization of the book:

1. Belief in the potential for human beings to do great work together. The articulation of authentic intended outcomes and agreements, logistical organization, and ongoing monitoring of progress make it possible.

2. Belief in the power of tools to support our best work. Structures, protocols, and routines provide frameworks for productive collaborative experiences that include all perspectives, bring in new ideas, and lead to application.

3. Belief in working from the inside out. Planning guided by identified needs of the people doing the work and their perceptions of what will help them achieve their intended outcome ensure commitment and relevance.

Ways to Use This Book

In some situations, working and learning together can be a simple effort, such as when you have one clear task, a small group in agreement, and sufficient resources. However, in the context of complex school systems, there are often numerous obstacles to navigate. The tools presented here were developed over many years of working with teachers and administrators to provide simple and straightforward steps that support increasing teacher efficacy while navigating the logistical, habitual, and cultural complexities of school life.

The book is organized to allow multiple ways to access the resources. Tools include graphic organizers, planning guides, agendas, protocols and structures, activities, forms, and checklists to support application. These documents may be reproduced as they are presented, adapted, or used as a base from which you develop your own materials.

You could use the book as a road map to follow sequentially or flip through to find what suits your needs for particular purposes within the context you have already established. Either way, you will find these special features designed to help you quickly determine essential aspects of each tool so you can judge if it will work for you:

◆ **Aim:** What you can accomplish with the use of a particular tool

◆ **Considerations:** Key ideas and thinking to provide understanding so you can make best use of a tool

◆ **Guidelines and Activities:** Actions to take, reproducible materials, and a walk-through for application

◆ **Troubleshooting:** Tips to help you address and sometimes prevent potential problems

◆ **To Teachers:** Examples and ideas that address teachers directly

Restoring the Heart

The success of any systematic plan, framework, or structure ultimately depends on the attitudes, engagement, and commitment of the people charged with implementation.

As I think about my recent years of learning with colleagues, I am reminded of a Bollywood movie with a large cast, vivid colors, passions, tensions, and complex dance productions that call forth but do not fall into chaos. I see so many characters sitting around tables in various kinds of rooms, crammed into too-small principals' offices, huddled in large school libraries, bursting with passionate reactions in hallways after observing in classrooms. I see earnest faces turned to a colleague who is expressing a complex idea that captures the essence of a student's learning, and note the smiles and grimaces as people consider solutions for knotty problems. I also see teachers return to their classrooms with broader perspectives and a renewed enthusiasm and sense of community.

Inside I am nearly singing, "Can you believe this is happening? Can you believe we are getting this time to explore and delve and discover together? Can you believe the honesty and brilliance we're hearing?" And at the end of nearly every meeting, at least one person offers a Bollywood happy ending with a sigh, exclaiming, "This is the best professional development we have ever had."

PART I: FOUNDATIONS

Birds, fish and horses in a group know how to move or change direction at exactly the same time. It is because every member of the flock, school, or herd is aware of what the leader is focusing on. Focus is what allows a herd to perform its primary function, which is to act as one unit. The purpose of the herd is to be and act as a whole. A single unit composed of many is intimidating and confusing to predators. By becoming "one with" the others, each individual enjoys the safety that comes from being a part of a larger whole.

— GaWaNi Pony Boy

I assume that horses and fish automatically work as a group, with no one having to make special arrangements or accommodations for their unified focus and actions to occur. My views of human beings indicate that it usually takes thoughtful preparation to create the conditions for individuals to work in unity with common purpose and focus, and that's what this section will address.

While a book has to physically present one idea at a time in a sequential and linear layout, my experience in schools is that we are usually taking several steps and covering multiple bases at one time. The next three chapters offer ideas for laying a solid foundation. Since we can't do everything all at once, decide what makes sense for you in your time and place, knowing that with your focus in mind, you can continually build on the previous step you have taken.

CHAPTER 1
SETTING THE TONE

People can only support what they help to create.
— community organizing adage

Most of my career in education has been focused on professional learning, and when I think back through all the years of success and failures, I see a clear common thread. The times I have seen lasting change as a result of my work with anyone, be it a principal or teacher, district administrator, or community member, happened when the people who had a stake in the outcome were "at the table," with ownership and responsibility for the work, the learning, and the outcomes shared equitably among the members of the group.

Where this kind of collaborative inquiry has taken hold as part of how a school operates, the atmosphere for teacher commitment and practice shimmers with life and growth. I believe this difference comes from having educators at the helm rather than as passengers.

Picture a group of teachers gathered in a library, conference room, or a classroom, with a shared focus on learning and improving instruction. They may be a group that meets only once or a few times to address a discrete, narrow goal, or they may continue from year to year with a broader purpose or for ongoing support and learning. Often these are groups that are already identified, such as department or grade-level teams, or a whole-school faculty, using meeting or in-service time to have focused conversations.

During their time together, the group might be focused on a particular task or challenge, or they could be discussing theoretical issues and professional literature, analyzing data and fine-tuning plans in response to the data, exploring essential questions about teaching and learning, observing in classrooms, walking through schools, focusing on individual children. They may offer one another feedback, strategies, ideas, and support for concrete issues, plans, or questions. Most often, though not always, someone is acting as a facilitator or leader, holding responsibility for the meetings. Eventually, others may step forward to share responsibility for planning, leading, and facilitating.

While there is unlimited variety in the specifics of how teachers can work and learn together, certain underlying principles apply in nearly all variations for smooth functioning and achievement of desired outcomes. Throughout this book, you will find tools and explanations based on these principles. But first there are a few basic details that establish a tone for authentic and relevant work.

AIM: PLANNING FOR SHARED OWNERSHIP AND RESPONSIBILITY

When I am planning, it helps me to get a physical picture in my mind of the best-case scenario of the group working together. I imagine us in the room sitting so that everyone is visible and in an equal position to talk to the rest of the group. This may well seem like a minor or obvious step but it is often overlooked, with unfortunate consequences.

When the physical space is the right size and shape, this is a simple task that doesn't require much thinking on my part; I just move chairs into a circle or around a table. However, we are often in crowded rooms, with immovable tables, echoing acoustics, or too many participants for a comfortable circle. Then I use that picture in my mind to guide me in figuring out alternative arrangements that still support conversation and community as I imagine it, so the focal point is in the center of the group and participants can talk with one another.

WHO WILL BE THERE?

Who will be sitting in that circle is another basic and crucial detail that sets the tone for the group's functioning. Success for your group endeavor is most likely when everyone involved is invested and engaged. There are many choices to make in bringing people to that circle, mostly having to do with whether they are invited, selected, or mandated to participate.

Everything will be harder if people feel coerced or, on the other hand, if they know colleagues feel excluded. The challenge in every situation is to find a way to bring people to a place of ownership and shared responsibility.

When the members of the group are predetermined, such as in grade-level, department, or content-area teams, you will often also have predeter-

TROUBLESHOOTING: BRINGING OUTSIDERS INTO THE CIRCLE

Some people purposely sit outside the circle, either because they don't want to participate or they don't see a space for themselves. The impact on the rest of the group can be subtle or overt, but it is always detrimental. I have learned that their behavior will inevitably be "outside the circle," with side conversations or in a non-participant role. You might say, "We want to make sure everyone is a part of this conversation. We can make room." This is a clear message that everyone's participation is expected, and necessary.

mined goals and tasks to accomplish. When this is the case, you can still offer an invitation to engage in work that is directly linked to a benefit for classrooms, students, and school.

When membership needs to be determined, such as in leadership teams or steering committees, study or book groups, inquiry groups, or student referral teams, it is usually desirable to err on the side of inclusion, with an open invitation that communicates an implicit message to the community that everyone's contribution is welcome, rather than favoring a chosen few who are deemed worthy. Then, those who join commit to the process and goal, and nonparticipants choose to leave it to their colleagues.

With completely voluntary groups, you are likely to end up with a group of kindred spirits, safe with one another, willing to take risks, eager to talk and build momentum to a common goal.

On the other hand, there is a richness and learning that arises from the discomfort and dissonance of members of a diverse group who represent different grade levels, schools of thought, backgrounds, or personal styles. You can hear and learn things you may never have thought of, creating stronger connections in your community.

You might want to encourage specific people to join. Think about those who have most at stake with what could be accomplished and approach them directly. Talk about this as a special opportunity, a gift provided by the PTA, the district, or the principal to get together. Talk about the purpose of the group. Ask people to give it a try by coming to at least the first, possibly also the second, meeting with the option to continue or not.

With ongoing projects, allow for times to open to new members. New members will keep groups from becoming insular, cut off from the rest of the school and new perspectives, exclusive in their bond. When there is a risk of taking backward steps with people who have not shared foundational activities, built relationships, or gathered collective knowledge, establish ways to bring new members into the group through summaries of what you have done and discussed to date.

When determining who will be in the group, you might run into decisions about the ideal size for achieving your purpose, because size does matter. The smaller the group, the more visible each person is, and the less risky it is for people to speak up. Intimacy and trust are more easily and quickly developed. With fewer people, consensus on decisions and plans may take less time. It also takes less time for everyone to be heard in a discussion or activity. However, you decrease your chances of having multiple perspectives represented, achieving school-wide impact, and benefiting from the energy of disagreement and resolution. To address this, you can bring in outside perspectives through readings, visitors, and stories. You can spread the impact if each member of the group commits to talking with his team or at least one colleague.

As you increase the number of participants, you have the potential for more perspectives and impact, yet you run into the challenge of making sure every perspective is heard, that everyone is comfortable enough to speak up. You might find a need for more structures that give everyone a chance to speak, particularly small-group experiences. Breaking into smaller groups or dyads at times allows participants to experience the intimacy of a smaller conversation. Circles of more than 25 can feel powerful but take on a different feeling, as people end up sitting relatively far away from each other, with a big empty space in the middle. Plan from the beginning to bring each person's voice "into the room." (See Chapter 4.)

Another decision you might face is whether the principal or other administrator should be part of the group—whether you need that person's expertise, point of view, or influence, or whether those very things will impede the group's open conversations. If the principal is not there, keep her informed and involved. District administrators will often be interested, and even provide concrete support, if they see what you do as a possible model for others to follow. If you are a district coach, you probably have systems in place to keep your supervisor aware of your work and the results you are getting. Informal comments and brief anecdotes pique people's curiosity to hear more. Written reports are useful for getting attention and making clear statements.

Though you will hold primary responsibility for the ongoing leadership and facilitation of the group work, within each meeting or activity look for opportunities to gradually release that responsibility to members of the group for authentically shared and distributed ownership.

AIM: ESTABLISHING WILLINGNESS, NOT RESISTANCE

"Quit moaning, Carrie!" she says sharply. "I want you to think *about this while I'm gone. Nobody's saying you got to go there. But you got to* imagine *going there. Otherwise you'll not have a hold of your choices. I got no ax to grind—what you decide is your own private business. But if you decide to give it a shot, I'd say it's time to make your move. You're as ready as you're going to get."*

— Mary Ann Taylor-Hall, *Come and Go, Molly Snow*

When you are doing anything new or different, resistance and concern are natural responses not to be dismissed, but rather to be expected, accepted, and planned for and addressed in ways that are still respectful and collaborative in their nature.

The Managing Complex Change model (Fig. 1-1), developed by Stephen Ambrose, provides a simple matrix that identifies essential elements necessary for change, linked to identifiable reactions that occur when a specific element is lacking. This is very useful for planning to get everything necessary in place as well as providing clues for revising when you hit reactions that block progress. Refer to the matrix to see what is missing and figure out what you can do.

CONSIDERATIONS

Some principals distribute a copy of this matrix to the teachers at each faculty meeting or in-service day as a way to gather data to inform subsequent plans for support and meetings. Each teacher self-identifies her reaction(s), the category, and specifics of what she needs in order to move forward.

Use the blank form (Fig. 1-2) to develop plans that include all necessary elements. If you find there's an element missing from your plan, take the opportunity to revise it before putting it into action.

FIGURE 1-1

MANAGING COMPLEX CHANGE

	+	Skills	+	Incentives	+	Resources	+	Action Plan	=	CONFUSION
Vision	+		+	Incentives	+	Resources	+	Action Plan	=	ANXIETY
Vision	+	Skills	+		+	Resources	+	Action Plan	=	RESISTANCE
Vision	+	Skills	+	Incentives	+		+	Action Plan	=	FRUSTRATION
Vision	+	Skills	+	Incentives	+	Resources	+		=	TREADMILL
Vision	+	Skills	+	Incentives	+	Resources	+	Action Plan	=	CHANGE

Adapted from Ambrose 1987

Tools for Leaders © 2007 by Marjorie Larner, Scholastic Professional

FIGURE 1-2: ORGANIZER

PLANNING FOR COMPLEX CHANGE

Vision	Skills	Incentives	Resources	Action Plan	CHANGE

AIM: DEFINING AND DISTRIBUTING ROLES AND RESPONSIBILITIES

To punish me for my contempt for authority, fate made me an authority myself.
—Albert Einstein

When roles and responsibilities are clearly laid out, not only are people more comfortable joining in and taking on tasks, it is also possible for them to see what it would take to grow into a new role, to try out something they haven't attempted before. Especially when you have a lot to accomplish in a short period of time, explicit expectations of each person's responsibilities provide the backbone of an efficient, short-term collaborative inquiry project. Furthermore, you can see how each person's particular skills and commitment contribute to the smooth functioning of the group. With this clarity, everyone has the opportunity to share responsibility and influence.

CONSIDERATIONS

Reasonable and explicit expectations provide guidelines so that each person has an idea of what he or she is agreeing to do. As with any checklist (Fig. 1-3), every item might not be applicable every time, and there could be times when you will add new items.

FIGURE 1-3

ROLES AND RESPONSIBILITIES

The **FACILITATOR** is an observer and a witness, supporting the group's efforts, synthesizing the content of each discussion, making connections to the larger context, and bringing together ideas from different groups.

FACILITATOR	RESPONSIBILITIES
	Help the group achieve goals and stick to agreed-upon norms and agenda
	Scaffold activities and discussions to construct meaning/learning
	Provide what will make participants comfortable—breaks, refreshments, room temperature, etc.
	Talk with presenters, and teachers who will be observed or take a leadership role in other ways, to help them prepare

PARTICIPANTS share responsibility for speaking up about the direction of the group, make a commitment to apply new learning, and remain open to new ideas and perceptions.

PARTICIPANTS	RESPONSIBILITIES
	Share experiences, questions, expertise, and knowledge
	Seek new ideas and skills through reading and listening
	Take time from other obligations to make this work a priority
	Speak up and share responsibility for the direction and success of the group

ADMINISTRATORS believe in the power of this process to impact students' educational experience, ask hard questions, and engage in focused discussions about their own practices.

ADMINISTRATORS	RESPONSIBILITIES
	Articulate the connection of the group's work to their vision for the school
	Provide funding—if a facilitator needs payment, food, or release time for teachers
	Show deep interest and belief in what the group is discovering; join when appropriate
	Support ideas for change that come out of the group's exploration—help with implementation and dissemination of the learning to other groups

AIM: WORKING WITH STRENGTHS AND PREFERENCES

Treat people as if they were what they ought to be, and help them become what
they are capable of being.
—Johann von Goethe

Within each of the three general categories of participants, there is room for the unique contributions of each individual, as well as room to shift responsibilities among members of the group. The list is a guideline from which you can match tasks with the individual styles and preferences of the people involved. For some people the concrete items that can be scratched off a list are desirable tasks to take on, and it is good to know who can be relied on to take responsibility for each of these small, crucial tasks. For others, tending to how everyone is feeling, or taking notes, or setting up schedules is an easy responsibility to meet.

CONSIDERATIONS

The Compass Activity (Fig. 1-4) provides a simple framework and a lively process to identify strengths and preferences related to working collaboratively. It is a powerful opening activity with almost any group, as it gives people time to talk with others like themselves in small affinity groups and then share their characteristics with other groups.

When you participate in this activity, you increase your awareness of what comes naturally to you, what you have to work harder to accomplish, and where you find frustration. This awareness of your own style and also of the styles of your colleagues can help you work together to use strengths and preferences to best advantage.

This protocol is designed for a large group of at least 12 people. It is a powerful activity to use with the whole faculty early in the school year, serving as an opportunity to establish the foundation for future collaboration as you learn more about each person's ways of working.

With a smaller group, you could have an informal conversation about where each of you might place yourself, what strengths and challenges you experience, and how your attributes affect your work together in this group and in your other teams. This small-group discussion would be a good way for you to get prepared to facilitate a larger group in this activity.

FIGURE 1-4: ACTIVITY

Compass Activity
(aka Four Corners, or North South East West)

PURPOSE: To better understand preferences in group work

INTRODUCTION: Have you ever left a meeting and said to your colleague, "That was the best meeting ever," and your colleague turns in shock and says, "I thought it was a waste of time"? There is a good reason why your great meeting is someone else's horror show. We all have different ways that work for us in collaborative settings, and it is helpful to be aware of what our preferences are as well as the preferences of those with whom we will be working.

STEPS (Facilitator briefly introduces the steps of this activity.)

1. The room is set up with four signs: North: Action; South: Caring; East: Vision; and West: Structure. Post blank chart paper by each sign.

2. Introduce each of the signs, elaborating on the four essential elements of group work. Acknowledge that few of us are only one way, but for this exercise, encourage participants to choose a predominant preference. Assure them they won't have to stay in that "box" forever, just for the duration of this exercise, so whichever direction they land in, there will be something to learn.

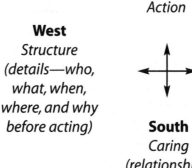

North
Action

West
*Structure
(details—who,
what, when,
where, and why
before acting)*

East
*Vision
(big picture)*

South
*Caring
(relationships)*

3. Invite people to move to the corner that best represents the element most essential—what comes easiest, most naturally—to them in group work. Suggest they pick just one and see what they learn in that discussion.

4. The task of each group is to respond to a set of questions that are posted or distributed on a sheet of paper. In each group, ask for a volunteer to record responses and a reporter to present back to the larger group. Basic set of questions:
   ◆ What are the strengths of your preferred style?
   ◆ What are the limitations?
   ◆ What do you want others to know about you?
   ◆ What would you choose for a mascot (symbol, animal, person, etc.) to represent your style?
   ◆ What is your motto?

5. After 10 to 15 minutes of small-group discussion, each group explains the strengths and limitations of their element to the whole group. Offer applause after each group presents, a gesture of appreciation for who they are and what they bring.

Tools for Leaders © 2007 Marjorie Larner, Scholastic Professional

FIGURE 1-4, PAGE 2

6. The facilitator leads the group in a discussion of the presentations. You might simply start out and ask, "What did you notice?" People will usually talk about how their group worked together, how presentations reflected their style (e.g., West's chart was very neat and organized, North went first, etc.), and what happens in a group if one of the styles is not present and whether someone else can step up to fill it in.

Additional points for the facilitator to consider introducing to the conversation:

◆ It is important to acknowledge the strength of each element as well as the potential downsides of each one when taken too far. Provide a strong caution to avoid negative comments or jokes about the style preferences of others. When participants make comments, even in jest, about where their colleagues place themselves, it brings a negative flavor to the exercise rather than the collaborative spirit it is intended to develop.

◆ Look at the distribution in the four groups and ask how this will affect the functioning of the whole group. Will there be enough people to take care of each aspect of a group's operations? If it is lopsided, ask what that might mean for the group. For example, a group with nearly everyone in **vision**, with a few people in **action** and **caring**, and with no one at all in **structure** will have to work conscientiously together to be sure they develop some workable structures that lead to action. If **caring** is small, there may need to be more care taken that everyone is heard and that food and drink are provided for lunch meetings.

◆ Consider which roles and responsibilities for collaborative work will be most comfortable and which will be most of a stretch for you given your style.

VARIATIONS:

◆ Offer an opportunity for people to move to their second choice for a brief discussion of the interaction of their two styles, or in the direction that they see as opposite to their preference, and discuss what aspect of that style they have in them.

◆ If you are looking specifically at developing deeper working relationships, perhaps on a team, you could ask:
   What group agreements are most important to your style of working?
   What are you most satisfied doing?
   What do you find most difficult to participate in?
   If you had your way, _____?

◆ To offer a focus on issues of equity, include questions such as:
   What part does your background (cultural, ethnic, racial, socioeconomic, native language, gender, etc.) play in the style you prefer?
   What challenges arise for you with this preference as a result of your background?
   How does this preference align with expectations of how you behave according to your background?

Developed in the field by educators affiliated with the National School Reform Faculty (NSRF); see Recommended Web Sites and Resources, p. 171

FIELD NOTES

The ways that people in your group see and carry out their tasks will take on variety and color from their personalities and styles, as well as from the context within which you are working.

As an example of how the items on these lists look when brought to life, Fig. 1-5 shares a plan for division of responsibility for a short-term project with language arts teachers. The goal for this project was to strengthen adherence to an agreed-upon, well-defined instruction-

FIGURE 1-5

Example of Shared Responsibilities

The principal defined her primary role as the one to "hold the pedal to the metal" through these responsibilities:

◆ Individual conferences with teachers

◆ Official teacher evaluations that include participation in this effort

◆ Reliable classroom coverage during the project

◆ Clear articulation of outcomes and goals

The in-school literacy coach's role was to provide ongoing and continuous support and conversation through these responsibilities:

◆ Meetings with teachers in between observations; feedback, co-teaching; demonstration lessons and planning support

◆ Scaffolds, organizers, and concrete suggestions for how to organize and keep records

The external coach's role was to facilitate the process, hold the big picture, and provide resources through these responsibilities:

◆ Structures, protocols, texts, and materials for each step

◆ Explicitly articulated overview of the process

◆ Documentation, notes, and reports

Each teacher participant's role was to actively engage in exploration, discovery, and application of new ideas through these responsibilities:

◆ Commitment to work toward a self-identified goal within the plan

◆ Observations in their own classroom and of colleagues in their classrooms

◆ Support and feedback to colleagues

◆ Sharing (learning and challenges) with other teachers in the building about the project

al model. In order for teachers to share ownership and responsibility even when working within a mandate, it proved crucial to balance support with pressure, honor individual choice within the predetermined parameters, respect teachers' creativity, and provide leadership.

Responsibilities were divided among the principal, three teachers, an in-building coach, and me, the external coach. The assistant principal and secretaries filled in for the principal when her attention was on this group.

At the end of the project, when we met to debrief the ups and downs and changes that had occurred over the six weeks, Mary Lynn Brown, one of the language arts teachers, reflected, "Teaching is not a solitary activity anymore."

CHAPTER 2
LOGISTICS

If you have built castles in the air, your work need not be lost; that is where they should be.
Now put foundations under them.
— Henry David Thoreau

Joy Hood, a former principal who now coaches other principals leading their schools through transitions, describes the feeling of change as that moment when a trapeze artist lets go of one swinging bar and hasn't yet grabbed the new one. When we are in that moment of letting go of an old idea or approach before we have a solid grasp on the new one, when we are in that limbo between letting go of one bar and grabbing onto the new bar, it can be vital to know there is a net when the bar is out of reach. Carefully managed logistics are the net. And it is pretty obvious when the net is missing.

Well-managed logistics lead to a feeling of safety, appreciation, and support among group members. No matter how compelling the purpose for a group to meet, if provisions for time, money, communications, and responsibilities are lacking, confusing, or frustrating, participants are likely to grumble, be distracted, and get less out of the meetings. Attending to little things that may seem trivial—like who will carry heavy bottles of water into the building, who will move chairs and make copies—actually lays a foundation for achieving results.

When you see logistics for what they are—items on a checklist or "the planning and implementation of a complex task"—they become a strength that makes thoughtful work possible.

OVERALL MANAGEMENT

Logistical efficiency requires thinking and planning ahead, when possible, walking through each step in your mind to imagine every detail. To create a checklist (see Fig. 2-1), you could start with questions that surface as you think about the meeting. You can keep it in the form of a list or turn it into a timeline.

FIGURE 2-1: ORGANIZER

CHECKLIST FOR OVERALL LOGISTICAL MANAGEMENT

COMMUNICATIONS

	WHAT	WHO	WHEN
With participants			
With administrators			
With others (specify)			

RESOURCES

Funding (subs, facilitators, space)			
Time (release, stipends for outside-of-school)			
Materials (books, journals, copies)			

Tools for Leaders © 2007 Marjorie Larner, Scholastic Professional

QUESTIONS TO CONSIDER

How far is parking from the building (an important question to consider when you're carrying in supplies)? Will you need a cart? How will the room be arranged when the group arrives, and who will move chairs into place and return them to their original positions? Will participants be able to sit in a circle so you can all see each other and talk as a group? Will space and acoustics allow you to break into smaller groups? Who will make copies? Who makes sure everyone knows date, time, and place? Who creates the working agenda for each meeting? Who keeps notes or writes reports?

FUNDING

Over the years I have seen magic worked by determined principals and teachers who know how to state their case and build allies to support their projects. They have taught me not to give up when someone tells me there is no money.

With the right kind of contacts and relationships, and a clear description of expected results for your project, you might find open pockets.

BRAINSTORM SOURCES OF SUPPORT

Take some time to imagine and brainstorm all the possible sources for financial support. Think of people you have worked with in the past who may now be in a position to access funds or have contacts who can help. Enlist help from your principal, other coaches, and/or your immediate supervisor in the district. You may think of many more sources than I have included here.

◆ Small grants are often quite accessible from local foundations, community education funds, and local education funds. Ask other people in the field and look on Web sites of nonprofits to see who their funding agents are. Many educational associations and e-mail newsletters provide lists of currently available grants.

◆ Large grants often call for some specialized skill and/or connections to get access to potential funding partners. Many districts have employees whose primary responsibility is writing those grants and developing these relationships. They will often help you with your project, particularly when it is a group undertaking with the potential to benefit more children or schools in the district.

◆ Funding agencies or foundations not usually associated with educational initiatives might still share an interest in your topic, process, or results. This allows you an opportunity to make a strong case for the value of a partnership with a project that benefits children and their education.

- Active PTAs or PTOs often provide funds for purposes promoted by teachers, as a means of contributing to their children's educational experience. Make an explicit connection for them between support for your project and the benefit for their children.
- Grant writers are sometimes willing to offer consultation and advice as a community service. You may find aspiring grant writers in your parent community who want to gain experience by working with you on a proposal.

TIME

*The value of life lies not in the length of days, but in the use we make of them;
a man may live long yet live very little.*
— Michel de Montaigne

The most common reasons I hear cited for not doing something: "There is no time . . . to provide for teachers to talk with each other." "There is no time . . . for teachers to be out of their classrooms." "There is no time . . . to do anything but what directly prepares students for achievement on tests." And yet, you also hear that "it" has to happen now and "it" has to happen fast. "There is no time . . . to wait for increased test scores or to narrow the achievement gap." I also hear that kids must gain skills and understandings each day they spend in school and there is no time to wait to make that happen.

Time may seem like a static barrier to us, yet with careful planning and use of resources, you can find time to do what needs to be done.

OPTIONS TO CONSIDER
Standing back and looking at obstacles dispassionately often leads to seeing new solutions to big problems such as how to cover classes with minimal disruption and minimal reliance on substitute teachers.

Teachers and administrators find ingenious solutions for classrooms to be covered. Start by asking group members, "How would you like to do this? Which of these options do you like or can you think of others?" You might hear suggestions such as these:

TROUBLESHOOTING: JUSTIFY YOUR REQUEST

I hear complaints about continual professional development for teachers that takes time and resources away from teaching. In response, I suggest that teaching is not a finite skill that you can learn once and for all. There is always more to learn, and when the learning is directly connected to the particular children in your building, you can be confident it will make a difference in your classrooms. Do our critics question why their doctor is required to go to conferences to learn the latest methodologies and protocols? Would they want teachers to stop learning more about how best to serve children?

- Meet during the non-classroom time that already exists, such as planning time, team meetings, faculty meetings.
- Combine two classrooms for one period, so that one teacher works with all the students and the other can be released.
- Ask adults (administrators, counselors, parents) who are not tied to a classroom if they would be able and willing to take a classroom for a short period of time. They are often glad to spend time with students in a classroom setting.
- Hire a roving substitute teacher who covers classes for a staggered meeting schedule.

Scheduling

Settling on times to do your work always seems to come down to seeing where to take the time with the least negative impact on teachers' responsibilities, whether it is during planning, or teaching, or before or after school. Some groups are more complicated to schedule than others, and the more schedules you are accommodating, the more complicated it becomes, so the more urgent it is to come up with those dates well in advance.

Schedule dates when you and your team members are face to face, whenever possible. I have learned from sad experience that scheduling through e-mail inevitably leads to confusion as e-mails fly back and forth and people lose track of sequence and decisions.

If you can't avoid scheduling via e-mail, include specific choices and a standard format for people to check off, and designate one person to keep track with an easy-to-use organizer. (See Fig. 2-2 and 2-3.) Just keep these templates ready on your computer to use whenever the need arises.

Troubleshooting: Commitments & Realities

When groups are large or you are meeting multiple times over a period of months rather than days or weeks, you might do well to plan for the inevitable missed meetings by having a process in place for people to find out what they've missed so they don't feel lost at the next meeting. Everyone can take responsibility for staying informed by reading notes or checking in with you or a colleague who did attend.

MAKING THE MOST OF THE TIME YOU HAVE
- To the best of your ability, plan your meetings for the amount of time, and only that amount, that you think people will be able to focus and concentrate.
- Vary the types of activities between the expected sitting and talking and experiential learning and chances to get up from chairs. It is hard to sit and talk productively for a whole day.
- Planning, decision making, and problem solving that must result in consensus and a product are often more exhausting than discovery and analysis that are more open-ended. When you draw up a

FIGURE 2-2: ORGANIZER

Excerpt from an e-mail for scheduling

Please let us know your availability for either or both of the dates below.

Date _____   yes_____   no_____

Date _____   yes_____   no_____

Other Comments:

Please RSVP by   day _____   date _____

We will schedule for when the most people can be there.

Looking forward to seeing you.

FIGURE 2-3: ORGANIZER

Scheduling Response Table

Name	Date of Response	Response

schedule, strike a balance through pacing and timing of different kinds of activity. It is hard to plan in the last 20 minutes of a long meeting when everyone is tired and ready to leave.

◆ There no longer seems to be any time of year when there isn't something especially demanding going on—from the first day of school to the holidays to preparing for the state test and intermittent district assessments to wrapping up the year. So you just have to accept what you can get. Starting your planning, or at least introducing the possibility of the project, at the beginning of the year, you can hook people's interest before they start drowning in the pace of the school year.

PRACTICAL COMMUNICATIONS

Education is when you read the fine print. Experience is what you get if you don't.
— Pete Seeger

I have walked into buildings with my arms loaded with copies and food to find that no one in the office knew we were meeting. Then I have wandered around looking for someone who knew where we were supposed to gather and could make sure that teachers were greeted and directed to our meeting.

After a few experiences like these, the risk of delegating seemed too great. But I knew that doing it all myself was out of the question, not only because it was too much for one person to do but also because it sends the message that I am the only one carrying responsibility and everyone else can be passive.

To ensure that the right people have the necessary information, create a checklist for a conversation, e-mail, or phone calls with the appropriate person so you each know what to expect and can share responsibilities. (See Fig. 2-4.) I have found there are many people who work in school offices who are very happy to provide for teachers' opportunities to work productively together.

EFFECTIVE E-MAILS

Our avenues of communication seem to be rapidly evolving, with the most visible change being an increased reliance on e-mail. With this, we need to think about how best to communicate through this medium.

I have labored over an e-mail with important information and a request for response and then waited in vain to hear back from people. Or even worse, later on, I sometimes receive complaints from people who say they didn't get the information, so they didn't have what they needed for the meeting, like lunch or pen and paper. I have to wonder,

Figure 2-4: ORGANIZER

Communications Checklist

Checklist Items	Yes	No	Not Required	Comments
Do the school secretary and all office administrators know about the meeting?				
If necessary, has the custodial staff or anyone else who needs to know been notified?				
Are personnel aware of the specific needs: electrical outlets, media, tables and chairs, time in the room, food being delivered or brought in, numbers of participants, clear directions on where to go?				
Is everyone, including participants, clear about the location for the meeting?				

did no one notice my e-mail even though I marked it highest priority? I may have to accept that my e-mail was not compelling enough for them to notice.

In truth, I shouldn't take it personally because I know that classroom teachers are spending their time with kids more than at computers. I accept this reality and limit the quantity and length of my e-mails as much as possible. I have given up worrying about people's inattentive habits, so I cover, and re-cover, all the bases. For instance, I'll send an article ahead of time to be read but also bring extra copies in case people have forgotten or mislaid it, so we can still have the conversation.

Ideally, this is one of the topics brought up in a discussion of agreements about how the community will work together. People can weigh in on the best ways to communicate, make commitments, and set expectations.

I have experimented with ways to write and send e-mails so that teachers read and respond to them when necessary, because I have found that in spite of the challenge, continuous brief communications keep the group connected between meetings.

◆ Keep messages and e-mails short. Two or three ideas in one e-mail are sufficient for busy recipients.

◆ Include notes and recommendations. Concrete plans and steps e-mailed along with reminders of the next meeting are more likely to be opened.

◆ Attend to timing and frequency. Participants are more likely to notice occasional, rather than constant, e-mails.

◆ Combine oral and written communications. Phone trees work with groups who are sharing responsibility.

◆ Add a very short, inspiring anecdote or joke or information from the field, preferably something participants could use with students or colleagues. People will come to expect something that will bring value to their day or work, at least a good feeling from reading your e-mails.

◆ Use one or two text features to help readers navigate and find important information. When there is a significant amount of information, boldface the topic in each paragraph. Create a consistent text structure for e-mails containing important information so that people grow accustomed to finding what they need.

◆ Put the information that requires a response at the beginning in case the recipients don't read to the end of the e-mail.

BASIC NEEDS

When peoples care for you and cry for you, they can straighten out your soul.
— Langston Hughes

Neila A. Connors has a book with an often-quoted title: *If You Don't Feed the Teachers, They Eat the Students! Guide to Success for Administrators and Teachers.* I add "or the facilitator." Because teachers often don't have the resources they could really use and they rarely take time to sit down and have lunch or take care of themselves, they appear to be able to get along without having their basic needs met. These teachers who spend their lives giving to others are especially grateful when we reach out to take care of them so they can concentrate on the work of teaching and learning.

Provide food, a comfortable meeting space, trustworthy classroom coverage—all the things that, when not provided, detract from participants' capacity to engage. Making explicit arrangements for who will attend to these details is worth the effort. When basic needs are filled and teachers are treated as though they matter, they will bond more quickly and work more effectively.

FOOD

I think we have all learned that even within a tight budget, a few dollars spent on snacks or drinks conveys a message that "we have thought about you and value your effort." Whether you are able to have food delivered or people have to bring their own, what is most important is letting people know what to expect so they can be prepared if they are to meet this need on their own.

BREAKS

If you can, let people know ahead of time when you will take breaks, so they can plan if they have to make a phone call or check something in the classroom. Be aware of the phenomenon that when you are facilitating or running a meeting, you might not notice a need for a break as much as participants in the group do.

TROUBLESHOOTING: UNEXPECTED SITUATIONS IN THE CLASSROOM

You want to aim for teachers to give their full attention to the task of the group. They need to know they are really and completely off duty, even if they are still in the building. If the substitute teacher is having trouble controlling a class, a parent needs attention, or a child splits a lip, administrators and office staff can be prepared to step in and protect this time for teachers.

FIELD NOTES

Just because you are a perfectionist does not mean you are perfect.
— Jack Nicholson

In spite of all the best efforts and intentions, there are times when you end up crowded into tiny rooms or moving two or three times in the course of a meeting, without the copies you need, sufficient uninterrupted time, or clear communications.

With a willing group, you can turn any negative into a positive—being cozy in a small space, or thinking of room changes as an opportunity to move your bodies, revive the discussion, and start fresh. Without copies, you draw from your own memories and ability to visualize. Without refreshments, you have license to eat junk food scavenged from school vending machines or your own candy stashes closeted for special occasions.

Acknowledging what cannot be controlled and doing what you can to compensate might be the closest to perfection you can get. Fortunately, if you stick with collaborating, over time you establish routines, everyone becomes accustomed to what needs to be done, and logistics become less of a challenge and more of a support that helps you all achieve your goals.

Chapter 3
Big-Picture Planning and Assessing

Nobody operating an automobile plant is interested in how many cars you produce; they want to know how many cars you produce that run.

—Deborah Meier

With all the stress on assessment in the last few years, I started noticing that every intentional action I took was in response to an assessment indicating that a new plan was needed to achieve my goal, in other words, to "produce cars that run." On the simplest level, every time I got in my car, it was because it was the best way to get where I needed to go. As a teacher, my lesson on short stories followed after I noticed that students' writing did not have logical sequencing, and with stories we could focus on beginning, middle, and end. Similarly, when I create an agenda or plan for working with teachers, I work backward from their needs and interests and desired outcomes. From the assessment, I see what my focus and actions need to be.

I know there are certain givens like state tests, district assessments, state and district standards, report cards, and so on. I also have my own dreams and hopes for students and their lives. I have to keep all of these integrated as I work with teachers and create plans for collaborative professional development.

Through the years, I have tried to find solid methods for holding it all—the numbers and the descriptions—in order to account for and be accountable to what can be measured as well as what can be perceived about students' progress and achievements. I have found a series of structures that provide scaffolding for dynamic, evolving plans and continuous, embedded assessments that can be woven into the normal operating routines of a school.

Aim: Developing an Initial Base Plan

As a first step, you might find it useful to develop your own basic overall picture of needs and plans with a series of questions to scaffold your initial thinking. (See Fig. 3-1.)

FIGURE 3-1: ORGANIZER

PLANNING SCAFFOLD

If all goes as you hope, what will be the outcome?	
Who needs to support and be part of this conversation?	
What resources will support this project?	
What will you do to develop collaborative relationships and habits?	
What knowledge, information, and data will inform and move the discussion and how will they be acquired?	
What results do you expect?	
Comments	

Tools for Leaders © 2007 Marjorie Larner, Scholastic Professional

AIM: MANAGING ONGOING PLANNING AND ASSESSMENT

With your basic plan providing a place to start, if you are looking at a plan that will continue over a period of time (more than a month or two), you could use the Futures Protocol (Fig. 3-2) and Asset Map Process (Fig. 3-3 and 3-4), so the bigger vision and ongoing plan is cocreated, and thus "owned," by the group.

The two activities provide scaffolding through the year for ongoing planning and assessment. Together they result in the following:

- ◆ A plan that is guided and implemented by the people who are affected by it
- ◆ A vehicle for combining information from multiple sources of data
- ◆ A system to look simultaneously at data on teacher and student change
- ◆ A method for using data on an ongoing basis to inform plans and practice
- ◆ A visual documentation to make plans and assessment public
- ◆ A way to keep the conversation going (Larner, 2004)

Summary of the steps from Backward Planning Through Ongoing Authentic Assessment:

- ◆ Include all invested members of the community.
- ◆ Create a detailed and concrete picture of desired outcomes.
- ◆ Identify current state with emphasis on evidence.
- ◆ Narrow to two or three priorities and actions to take.
- ◆ Collect and discuss data, from multiple sources, through the year to track progress.
- ◆ Allow for revision of priorities and plans.
- ◆ Repeat the process at the end of each year but in reverse order. Start with the Asset Map for discussion of where you are and where you'd like to go, and then use the Futures Protocol to create your revised plan.

BACKWARD PLANNING: FUTURES PROTOCOL

Scott Murphy developed this process for times when you are starting a new project and want to make sure you have articulated a full vision for your accomplishment as well as the steps to get you to that accomplishment. With this protocol, which takes about 60 to 75 minutes, depending on the size of the group, participants place themselves in a potential future, where they talk about the project as if it had successfully reached its greatest goals. Then they look back to where they started, as if it were the past (really their current reality). Then they connect these two perspectives with steps they imagine were taken to get to the dream future.

This protocol works well for discussing projects as specific as smooth, successful field trips where kids learn from the experience and build community to long-term projects such as whole-school improvement or a new plan for delivery of special education services

FIGURE 3-2: PROTOCOL

Futures Protocol (aka Back From the Future)

PURPOSE: To expand, clarify, and concretize the vision of what a group or individual is trying to accomplish. The time to use this protocol is in the early stages of creating a plan or project that has a specific end point and articulated goal.

YOU WILL NEED:
- Facilitator to help the group stay with the steps and not revert to the present
- Facilitator or another person to record ideas on chart

MATERIALS:
- Individual copies of the protocol or visible poster
- Chart paper and markers

BEFORE YOU BEGIN:
Post at least three pieces of chart paper side by side. Write the future end point date on the third sheet. This is where you will start. On the chart paper to the left, write the current date. Write "Steps" on the center sheet.

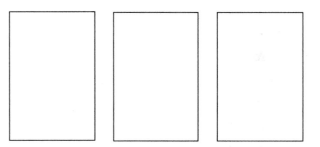

   If you have more than 15 participants, allow conversations in smaller groups of six or so for steps 1–3, with reporting back on the key points in the conversation to the whole group.

TIME: Approximately one hour

STEPS (Read through the steps before you begin.)

1. A group or individual describes a project. (5 minutes)
   - Include thoughts, desired outcome, concerns, challenges.
   - Identify an end point (specific date) toward which you would like to plan.
   Note: If this is a group or whole-school project, a spokesperson or leader might start the description and allow time for the group to contribute.
   Example: We are focusing on improving writing for students. We want to plan for what students who leave our school will know and be able to do as writers. It seems like a big project and we want the entire school to work together.

2. The whole group projects itself to that future and thoroughly describes what it looks like, sounds like, and feels like to have accomplished this endeavor. (10–15 minutes)
   Directions to group:
   - Talk in present tense (e.g., "We have a field trip program tied to the curriculum.")
   - Describe *what* is in this best-case scenario. Do not describe how.
   - Focus on the sights, sounds, behaviors, and feelings surrounding this accomplishment.

FIGURE 3-2, PAGE 2

Example: I see students writing all the time, everywhere in the building. My students ask for more writing time. Scores on state tests keep increasing. Students talk explicitly about assessing their writing according to the 6 Traits . . . .

3. The whole group looks back from the projected present and describes (using past tense) how it looked when it started. (5–10 minutes)

    Directions to group:

    ◆ Stay in the projected future and talk in past tense (e.g., "Remember when we felt our field trips were just add-ons that had nothing to do with our school day? We were worried about . . .")

    ◆ Think about issues, culture, conversations, teacher work, and student achievement/learning.

    ◆ Try to remain as tangible as possible.

    Example: Remember back in 2006 when test scores had been stagnant for years? Students were confused about paragraphs and complete sentences, even when they were toward the end of their years here. We had some star writers who were known by everyone in the building.

4. The whole group continues looking back from projected future and describes the steps they see that were taken to get from the starting place to the projected future they described in Step 2. (5-10 minutes)

    Directions to group:

    ◆ Talk in past tense.

    ◆ Directly relate the previous description of how it looked when it started.

    ◆ Consider discussing how, when, with what resources, and by whom things were accomplished.

    Example: I think everything changed for me when we read that article that helped us understand the essential components of the writing process. When we started our own writers' group, I remembered some of the steps of writing to include in my classroom. We started to develop a picture for writers at our school that we shared with kids and parents.

5. The whole group takes a minute to look at what is on the list and to celebrate what is on the list that is already in place.

6. The whole group identifies two or three priorities and related actions. (5 minutes)

    Examples:

    ◆ Develop clearly articulated outcomes.

    ◆ Decide on core best practice for teaching writing.

    ◆ Share successes and visit each other's classrooms.

    ◆ Plan to continue with the structure of the Asset Map Process (see Fig. 3-3) to support ongoing assessment and planning.

7. Debrief the process.

Developed by Scott Murphy

Tools for Leaders © 2007 Marjorie Larner, Scholastic Professional

FIGURE 3-3: ACTIVITY

Asset Map Process

PURPOSE: To provide a focus for ongoing discussion, revision, and visual documentation of commitments and progress

YOU WILL NEED: Facilitator to guide the process, keep time, maintain the focus, manage small group discussions, and facilitate whole-group discussion

MATERIALS:

◆ Sticky dots (about 1 inch in diameter works well, all one color; at a future time you may want to revisit and re-rank, at which time you will use a different color to distinguish where you were and where you are currently), enough for each teacher to have a set that matches the number of criteria on Asset Map

◆ Three copies per participant of Asset Map with 1–10 across the top (Fig. 3-5) on which you have circled either *School Culture*, *Faculty*, or *Students* (along the top) and have entered the criteria (along the side) drawn from previous discussion, such as from the Futures Protocol or other visioning process. (See Fig. 3-6 for examples of criteria.)

◆ Wall-size version of this Asset Map (approximately 3 feet by 4 feet)

◆ Wall-size Asset Map (3 feet by 4 feet) with months across the top (Fig. 3-7) on which you have entered the criteria along the side, for monitoring progress through the year

TIME: Two to three hours, depending on how many criteria you are considering; the process can be done in steps over the course of two or three meetings.

STEPS (Summarize the steps for the group before you begin.)

1. Each participant is given three copies of the Asset Map.

   Directions to participants: For each item, enter a rank of where you see the school on the scale of 1 to 10, with 1 being "rarely see evidence of this asset in place," to 10 being "see lots of examples of this in place." This is your impression of the whole school, if that is what is under discussion, not just your class or area of the building, but the whole of whatever is being considered in this vision. (10–15 minutes)

2. Teachers form small groups to discuss each item and their rankings on the chart. These groups function best when they include people who usually don't work together, people who will bring diverse perspectives to the conversation (e.g., from different grade levels, departments, roles in the school). Either direct participants to form such a group or preselect the groups to save time.

   Directions to participants: Your aim is to share and discuss evidence of why you ranked each criterion as you did. You might be influenced to change your rankings by others' evidence, or you might not. You may also have different understandings of what each criterion means in practice and this will come up in the discussion. It is not necessary to be certain of what each of these

FIGURE 3-3, PAGE 2

criteria means at this point. (30–45 minutes)

Example: "I see some students love to write, and write with both strong voice and conventions, but it is inconsistent, so I saw it as a 6." Someone else might respond, "I think everyone is working on this, so I gave it a 7."

3. Each person is given a set of sticky dots to match the number of criteria being assessed.

   Directions to participants: Place sticky dots indicating a ranking for each criterion on the posted Asset Map that has the criteria with numbers 1–10 at the top.

   This document is for your use and purposes only, not for anyone else's. It will not be made public so you don't have to worry about what you might reveal outside of this group.

4. The whole group gathers around and talks about what they see: patterns, frequency distribution such as scatter, cluster, contradictions, and so forth. As a facilitator, you can promote the exploratory nature of the discussion through the following means:

   ◆ Mirroring and paraphrasing what teachers are saying

   ◆ Encouraging exploration of definitions and meanings

   Questions to pose to participants to prompt this discussion:

   ◆ What do you notice?

   ◆ What, if any, connections exist among the three maps?

   ◆ Where is there agreement? Where is there disagreement?

   ◆ What surprises you?

   ◆ What assets are emerging as potential goals and why?

   ◆ How do the assets connect with and support standards?

5. From the information provided by the rankings and discussion, the group identifies areas to improve and chooses two or three areas of focus for either the semester or the year. This can be done as a whole group or you could offer time for small groups, perhaps grade-level teams or departments, to discuss and report back to the whole group.

6. The group discusses and identifies next steps.

   Directions to participants: If you used the Futures Protocol, return to Step 4 of that exercise for ideas to work from for these steps. Consider what is manageable.

   Example: To achieve a goal of articulating what each of the 6 Traits of Writing looks like, we will each create our own examples and talk about them with each other in our study group.

   If you have many steps, organize them along a timeline.

Adapted by Joy Hood and Marjorie Larner from Asset Map, developed by the Public Education and Business Coalition

Tools for Leaders © 2007 Marjorie Larner, Scholastic Professional

FIGURE 3-4: ACTIVITY

Asset Map Process Through the Year

"Teachers are regularly reminded of what they are striving to achieve and thus establish a habit of watching for evidence of progress or regress. This is authentic ongoing assessment. If they don't see progress one month, they can look at what was happening and remind themselves to re-focus. Like mile markers on the highway . . . the anecdotal records help track movement through the year. The map, posted in a common area such as the faculty lounge or hallway, is a visual reminder of goals that were set." (Larner, pp. 113–114)

At least once a month during the upcoming year, set aside time (e.g., the first 15–20 minutes at a faculty meeting) for each teacher to record and post anecdotes from observations and interactions that offer evidence of progress toward those two or three goals. Use the posted Asset Map that has months across the top. (See Fig. 3-7.)

STEPS

1. Volunteers are invited to share evidence (data, anecdotes, etc.) of progress toward meeting the goals.

2. Volunteers write their evidence on a sticky note with the date and post it in the appropriate box on the Asset Map.

   The evidence can come from diverse sources, such as these:

   ◆ Standardized test data

   ◆ District assessments with reading inventories and writing samples

   ◆ Records of attendance at parent conferences, back-to-school nights, family literacy nights, etc.

   ◆ Teacher's anecdotal records

   ◆ Observations of teaching and learning

   ◆ Notes from faculty meetings

   ◆ Comments from visitors, parents, students

   Examples:

   ◆ Kids talking to one another. One said, "Let me show you this paragraph where you can really hear my 'voice.'"

   ◆ Kids wrote for 45 minutes and asked for more.

   ◆ Scores on district writing sample rose 10 percent over last year.

3. Discuss as time allows

   In addition to tracking progress, this checking-in also serves as a way for teachers to share and celebrate successes and have a discussion about what works, from which everyone can benefit.

FIGURE 3-4, PAGE 2

Midyear and End-of-Year Assessments

When you are ready to step back again, such as at the beginning, middle, or end of the year, repeat the whole process to help you revisit, refocus, and revise your plan. Distribute sticky dots of another color (so you can see change) for ranking on the same Asset Map you used earlier (the one with 1–10 across the top).

STEPS AT A GLANCE

1. Individuals put their rankings on their personal copy of the Asset Map.

2. Meet in small groups to discuss.

3. Everyone puts their rankings on wall-size Asset Map with sticky dots.

QUESTIONS TO PROMPT DISCUSSION:

◆ If there are changes, what do you think they mean?

◆ Has your understanding of the criteria changed?

◆ How do you see priorities now?

◆ What would you do differently now?

4. Identify two or three goals to focus on for a set period of time.

5. Discuss actions to achieve goals.

6. Document evidence of progress toward goals on a monthly basis.

FIGURE 3–5: ORGANIZER

ASSET MAP

Circle one: School Culture   Faculty   Students

Assets evident when teaching and learning are aligned with vision and goals	1 Lowest	2	3	4	5	6	7	8	9	10 Highest

FIGURE 3-6

EXAMPLES OF ASSET MAP CRITERIA

ASSET MAP

Circle one: (School Culture) Faculty Students

Assets evident when teaching and learning are aligned with vision and goals	1 Lowest	2	3	4	5	6	7	8	9	10 Highest
Writing in many genres is posted in hallways.										
Student writing is read at assemblies and morning announcements.										
School publications feature student writing.										
Professional writers communicate with students.										

ASSET MAP

Circle one: School Culture (Faculty) Students

Assets evident when teaching and learning are aligned with vision and goals	1 Lowest	2	3	4	5	6	7	8	9	10 Highest
Are writers themselves										
Talk about writing										
Talk about writing with each other										
Use explicit descriptions of 6 Traits of Writing										

ASSET MAP

Circle one: School Culture Faculty (Students)

Assets evident when teaching and learning are aligned with vision and goals	1 Lowest	2	3	4	5	6	7	8	9	10 Highest
See and use writing as a tool for expression										
See and use writing as a tool for communication										
Are adept and flexible with writing in different genres										
Know and use conventions reliably										
Have stamina to write for long periods of time										
Can articulate and recognize writing that meets criteria of 6 Traits										

FIGURE 3-7: ORGANIZER

ASSET MAP THROUGH THE YEAR

Circle one: School Culture Faculty Students

Assets evident when teaching and learning are aligned with vision and goals	Sept.	Oct.	Nov.	Dec.	Jan.	Feb.	March	April	May

to focused projects such as a new direction for writing instruction.

Because this protocol requires participants to role-play and imagine themselves in another time, it can lead to laughter as people try to stay in the pretend place. It is important to have a facilitator to help the group stay with the steps and not revert to the present. I try to bring a lightheartedness and sense of fun to keep the group from taking the steps too seriously; even more important, when we're playful, our minds are more open to imagine new possibilities.

ONGOING AUTHENTIC ASSESSMENT: THE ASSET MAPPING PROCESS

Adapting a format originally developed to identify existing strengths in urban and rural communities, Ellin Keene and her colleagues at the Public Education and Business Coalition identified criteria from research on successful schools. They created a "map" with these criteria as a focus for faculty discussion and planning for the direction of school improvement.

When Ellin brought this map to use with the faculty at Foster Elementary School in Arvada, Colorado, then-principal Joy Hood added a step-by-step process to scaffold ongoing conversation that moves from current realities to priorities for improvement to tracking evidence of progress toward meeting those goals.

The Asset Mapping process has evolved over the years to meet the needs of the people using it. More and more often, I have heard requests from principals to include criteria drawn from their own schools' plans and standards in order to support the work they were already doing.

With this in mind, it seemed logical to combine the identification of a vision from the Futures Protocol with the assessment and planning structure of the Asset Map. This process, like the Futures Protocol, can be used on its own as long as you have some way of identifying agreed-upon criteria for discussion. (For further information on the original Asset Map go to www.pebc.org or see *Pathways: Charting a Course for Professional Learning* [Larner, 2004].)

FIELD NOTES

Watching Joy Hood facilitate this process that she has developed and used so frequently, I always learn some new subtle detail of the potential value that can be brought to teachers. Joy sees this as an opportunity to help teachers recognize their own increasing efficacy. When they bring in student data or anecdotes, she consistently asks them, "What did you do leading up to getting that student data or anecdote?" She also asks them to notice one another's successes, which are easier to report. She models noticing and documenting what teachers do connecting to student success. This changes the conversation and perspective for many teachers from their deficits and inadequacies to building on their own assets, within this process of building on the school's assets.

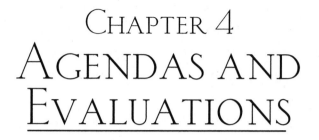

CHAPTER 4
AGENDAS AND EVALUATIONS

Good words do not last long unless they amount to something.
— Chief Joseph, Nez Percé nation

Before we get started, just like in the classroom, everyone wants to know, "What are you going to do?" And later, I hear, "So, how did it go?" The best thing that has happened over the years is settling on a simple framework to guide my planning and a variety of reflection/evaluation questions that have proven to elicit useful information for further planning.

AIM: CREATING AN EFFECTIVE AGENDA

Generally, the most successful agendas vary the degree of tight and loose structure to accommodate the different needs of individuals or of the topics and invite participants to actively engage in the process. I find it helpful to think about it as if I am providing the structure for this group's story and even borrow a story-planning tool from language arts classes (Fig. 4-1). Following the story planning, a graphic organizer is useful for formalizing the agenda (Fig. 4-2).

STEPS FOR PLANNING THE GROUP STORY

This sequence occurs in most activities and discussions with a beginning (make a connection and identify purpose and direction), middle (engage in learning and action), and end (recognize what you learned and identify next steps). This framework also helps me to hold the complete agenda in my mind while describing it to others so I don't have to keep referring to my notes during meetings.

1. **Introduction:** In a story you would start with introducing the characters, setting the scene, and establishing a reason for the reader to care. Start with a chance for each person to speak and be heard, whether it is a general check-in about "what is on your mind?" or a response to a specific question raised by the group. It is a chance for peo-

ple to make the transition from what they were doing before and for every voice to be in the room. In Chapter 5, you will find many options to use at the beginning.

2. **Theme:** In a story, you introduce a tension or a problem around which the plot revolves. With your group, identify issues, questions, dilemmas—whatever needs to be learned and addressed.

3. **Action:** This is the heart of the story, where the characters set an eventual resolution in motion, usually something that will change them in some way. Discuss reading or other sources of new knowledge and ideas, including implications for practice. This is what makes a meeting satisfying for participants, as they can feel their time is well spent. Again, in the next chapters, you will find many suggestions for processes and activities that may include a discussion, analysis, or exploration based on a text, workshop, classroom observation, or student work.

4. **Climax:** In a story, this is when the action reaches its peak. In your group, this is when the conversation is most focused and you're beginning to reach desired outcomes.

5. **Falling action:** The characters in the story can relax now; the action winds down as the problem has been resolved. In your work with teachers, this is when you identify questions to prompt reflection on the value and effectiveness of both the content and process of the meeting. Synthesize what you have accomplished and discussed, and offer the chance for participants to voice concerns, frustrations, and satisfaction, as well as to identify what they will take back to their classrooms, and to assess the connection between what they did at this one meeting and the collective vision.

6. **Resolution:** This is the happy ending, when all the loose ends are tied up. At the end, consider what you will do as a result of this meeting. Include details and logistics for next steps and ongoing support between meetings.

For the more detailed planning and notes to remember, many people use a table in order to create a clear visual outline and still allow for notes and comments both before and during the meeting (Fig. 4-2). The number of "boxes" you need in that table will vary to match your schedule.

AIM: ONGOING MONITORING OF PROGRESS

How are you going to know if you are accomplishing what needs to be accomplished with the plan you are using? Is it enough if everyone keeps coming? What if teachers like the meetings but there are no visible results for students? How are you going to prove to anyone that you are making a difference by meeting? How will you determine your direction and when it should change?

FIGURE 4-1: ORGANIZER

TEMPLATE FOR PLANNING MEETINGS

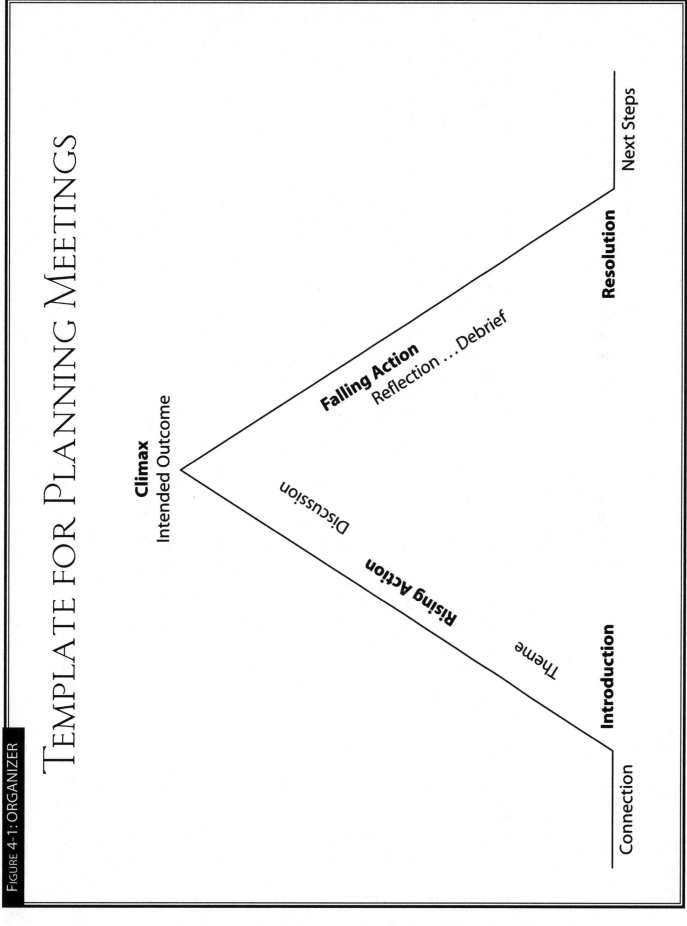

Climax
Intended Outcome

Falling Action
Reflection . . . Debrief

Resolution

Next Steps

Discussion

Rising Action

Theme

Introduction

Connection

FIGURE 4-2: ORGANIZER

AGENDA PLANNER

Agenda for:

Date:

Focus:

Time	Agenda	Comments/Notes

GET A COMPLETE PICTURE

What gets measured gets done.
— Margaret Spellings

The best and most beautiful things in the world cannot be seen or even touched. They must be felt in the heart.
— Helen Keller

Even though these two quotes appear to contradict each other, I would argue that both women are right, and there are probably even more perspectives to consider for a responsible view on how to monitor progress, whether for student or adult learning. Evaluation and assessment are so vital to informing and supporting our work that we can't afford to limit our view by trying to reduce educational questions to one and only one method for seeking information.

To align with the real world, we can attempt to include as many of the variables involved in drawing conclusions about human beings as we have available—both the measurable and the sensed. If we are in any way attempting to infer correlations, much less cause and effect, a standard research method of triangulation (which would include gathering data using three different instruments) is recommended to provide validity and generalizability. For instance, if your group has set a goal of improving writing, you might use sources such as these for gathering data:

◆ **Numerical data:** writing assessments from state tests, scored writing samples, enrollment patterns in advanced language arts classes, grades

◆ **Teacher reporting:** lesson and unit plans, teacher records and anecdotes, analysis of writing assignments, observations

◆ **Student self-reports:** interviews and surveys, self-assessments, reflections and journals

In Chapter 12, you will find a process for analyzing data from multiple sources, as well as an example of the process using data to inform changes in curriculum and instruction.

GATHERING DATA AND DRAWING MEANING FROM RESULTS

Another challenge in assessing and evaluating professional learning is sorting through the many variables in students' experiences in order to identify correlations between teacher learning and increased student learning. If we are to justify taking time and resources for doing this work together, we must be able to identify a connection between this work and results for student learning.

As you begin to gather data and evidence of results from your work together, it is helpful to conceptualize the flow of each step of the complex sequence from teacher learning through to student demonstration of learning:

teacher learning

↓

change in teacher thinking and knowledge base

↓

change in teacher practice

↓

evidence of change in student learning and knowledge base

↓

student performance/demonstration of learning

In many models of learning, reflection on learning and the implications for next steps are crucial parts of the cycle. Include time in the agenda, perhaps not at each meeting but on a regular basis, for individuals to respond to guiding questions that prompt reflection on the value and impact of the meetings. There are many methods to prompt and capture reflections, including these:

◆ Oral debriefs and reflections with a specific prompt, such as "What did we do today that I can take back to my students/faculty/colleagues?" "What did we do today that will have an impact on kids?" "What have I done differently since our last meeting?" The facilitator will need to take notes so that these are not lost.

◆ Written reflections in response to questions/prompts that are filled out at the meeting; provide a journal if possible. See suggestions for written evaluations at the end of the chapter.

◆ Written responses on e-mail or hard copy outside of the meeting as part of teachers' time commitment. Choose any two from the questions suggested above for oral or written responses, or make up your own.

◆ Anecdotes and observations recorded to provide evidence of change in teacher practice in classroom, or other change schoolwide.

◆ School data, teacher records, student interviews and surveys, and observations provide evidence of student change. Ask an expert on data analysis (e.g., the director of assessment for your district) to help you make meaning of the numbers and integrate different kinds of data (numbers, scores, surveys, observations).

◆ Record evidence of changes, using a table for an easy-to-see document from which to draw data for analysis and planning (Fig. 4-3). When you enter this data, think of what will be most useful and informative; include anecdotal as well as quantifiable information; and be specific (e.g., "Every student participated in discussion" or "Fifteen out of twenty students fully completed the writing assignment," as opposed to "Students were more interested in topic"). You could enlarge this form to a chart or project it on a screen for everyone to see during the discussion.

FIGURE 4-3: ORGANIZER

DOCUMENT TO TRACK LEARNING AND CHANGE

Date	What We Did	Teacher Learning	Teacher Change in Practice	Student Learning	Demonstration of Student Learning

REFLECTION AND EVALUATION FORMS

As a participant, I dread filling out evaluation forms and reflection sheets at the end of a workshop. However, as a facilitator or presenter, I love the routine of sitting down and reading participant reflections, so I am sensitive to what will lead participants to engage in the reflection/evaluation as opposed to just getting it done.

Depending on your purpose, your questions will be more or less evaluative or descriptive. If you do use numbers for ranking or rating an experience, offer an even number so people have to make a choice that falls to the positive or negative side, not in the middle. If you are asking questions for descriptive feedback, consider precisely what you need to know at that time to inform your planning and/or gather data.

These forms (Fig. 4-5 through 4-8) could be used any time you want to gather data about how the process is going: after a particular meeting, at midpoints in a long-term project, or as an end point assessment of a whole project. They are offered in a variety of formats that you can adapt for your own uses, or you can use them as they are offered. Consider maintaining an ongoing document of your work and progress, as seen on the figure below.

FIGURE 4-4

FACILITATOR REFLECTION AND EVALUATION

Participation	Who Participated	How they became involved
What we did	What worked	What didn't work
Learning	Learn more about	Support needed
Comments		

FIGURE 4-5: ORGANIZER

REFLECTION AND EVALUATION

How would you describe this experience to a colleague who had not participated?

Please give one concrete example of a way that your practice has changed as a result of your work with this collaborative group.

How have you or will you share this experience with colleagues?

What haven't we done that would further enhance your learning experience?

FIGURE 4-6: ORGANIZER

REFLECTION AND ASSESSMENT: FOCUS ON RESULTS

How did you grow as a teacher?

New thinking:

New knowledge:

Change in practice:

Change in student performance:

What worked for you in these meetings?

What would you do differently?

What else do you want to tell us?

Tools for Leaders © 2007 Marjorie Larner, Scholastic Professional

FIGURE 4-7: ORGANIZER

REFLECTION AND ASSESSMENT: FOCUS ON RESULTS

Project:

Date:

Your Name:

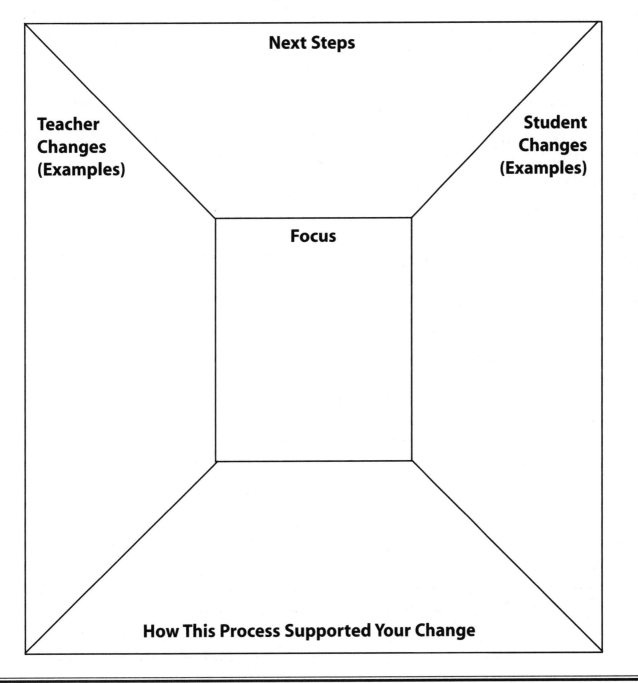

Next Steps

Teacher Changes (Examples)

Student Changes (Examples)

Focus

How This Process Supported Your Change

FIGURE 4-8: ORGANIZER

REFLECTION AND EVALUATION : INQUIRY WITH ESSENTIAL QUESTIONS

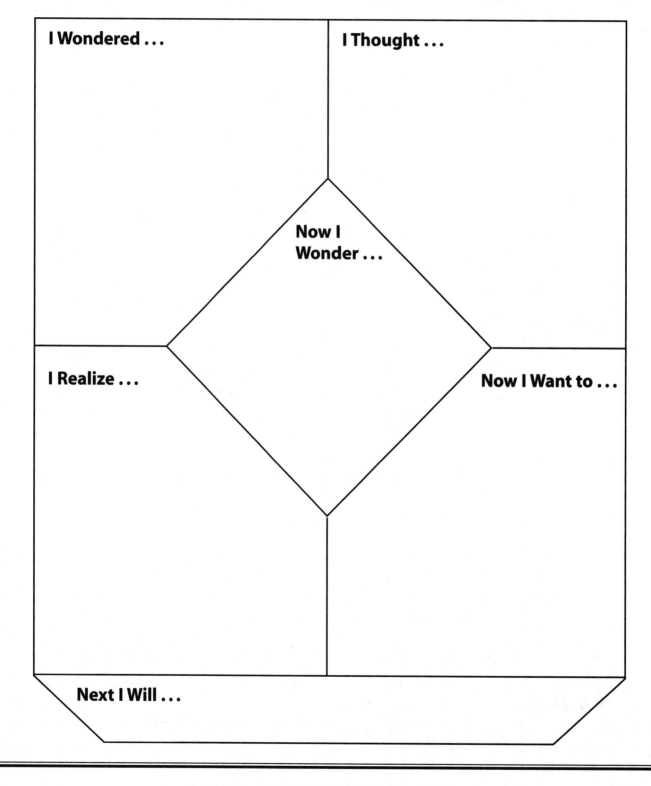

I Wondered . . .

I Thought . . .

Now I Wonder . . .

I Realize . . .

Now I Want to . . .

Next I Will . . .

Tools for Leaders © 2007 Marjorie Larner, Scholastic Professional

Field Notes

My hope is always that once teachers get a taste for working and learning together, it will become embedded in the way their school operates, rather than represent a novel idea that is dropped when something new comes along. My goal is that this work supports whatever else needs to be done. I have learned that sustaining collaborative efforts requires that we stop periodically to make sure we are on track and are making a difference with our efforts.

Three simple questions provide a framework to look at the overall project to date. For a more formalized discussion, especially when a written report is expected or desirable or when a group is having to make concrete plans, consider spending more time and taking notes to document the discussion.

- ◆ **What?:** What have we done and explored? (For example: discoveries about student learning and teacher practice, school structures.) Possible categories: what students get in school; what they keep; what they need.

- ◆ **So what?:** What have we learned and what does it mean for us and our students? (For example: implications for application from what we've learned.) Possible categories: what happens in school to support student success; what we do that supports their success; what we need to add/change.

- ◆ **Now what?:** What are our next steps? What will we do differently in response to what we have learned? For example: follow-up and reporting back on results of application. Possible categories: new and lingering questions to explore for further inquiry; continued collaborative learning, such as observations, interviews, reading, interventions in classrooms, and changes in school policy.

This discussion can have the flavor of reminiscing with friends or family after a trip or holiday has been shared, during which we get to relive the joys (and maybe struggles) of the experience, how it affected each of us, and what we want to do again (or never want to do again). Looking back together, remembering a common experience, reminds everyone of the value of connections and community.

PART II: THE HEART OF THE CONVERSATION

In traditional societies people are a valuable resource and the interrelations between them are carefully tended.

— Leinberger and Tucker

Many years ago, a principal directed me to help her teachers share their expertise with one another before I shared mine with them. She sent me off with a saying that she had heard from her grandmother, "Iron sharpens iron."

The structures and protocols presented in these chapters were developed by teachers, administrators, and coaches to support them in finding productive, efficient ways to work and learn together. When we use these tools we become more aware of the ways of behaving that we do naturally when we are at our best as members of a professional learning community: we take turns, listen with an open mind, speak our minds, and stay focused. The word *protocol* is used when referring to a specific and named process. *Structure* refers to the generic concept of frameworks, and so on.

I hear people talk about having the tough conversations, getting beyond congeniality and collegiality to true or deep collaboration that gets to the core of our work with students. If we are really going to go there, we need to make sure we have established patterns and habits of operating that are productive rather than destructive. We are, after all, human beings with history and emotions that can get triggered, for good or bad.

CHAPTER 5
BEGINNING THE CONVERSATION

Great minds have purposes, others have wishes.
— Washington Irving

When facing challenging situations in my work with adults, I often go back to what I've learned as a teacher. One of my favorite lessons with students is when we work on lead sentences to hook the reader. We identify explicit techniques to write those "grabber leads," such as starting with a question, dialogue, something surprising . . . well, the lists of what students have figured out is long. I think it is the same in a class, a meeting, professional development, anytime you want someone to join you. You have to hook your group members so they want to invest their time and effort.

What entices people to make time to meet with colleagues? Are they motivated by some promise of reward or by fear of negative consequences if they don't participate? Are they inspired by possibility and hope? Or are they engaged in the content or process of exploration, discovery, and results?

AIM: MOTIVATION

What mankind wants is not talent; it is purpose.
— Edward G. Bulwer-Lytton

I have watched many leaders over the years steer their schools through seemingly desperate situations. These effective leaders set a tone by the example of their own courage and determination to face a hard situation. The foundation of this courage was a high degree of motivation to achieve a goal or serve a purpose in which they deeply believed. They had their eyes on a destination they really wanted to reach and they were going to find a way to get there.

CONSIDERATIONS

Even if your school is under extreme pressure to show change or meet a specific goal, there is room for teachers to talk about their interpretations and intentions for meeting it. In fact, in this case, it is even more crucial that everyone has a chance to find a personal connection to the goal.

People still enter with their unique interpretations of why the group is meeting and why they, in particular, are there. You can establish precedents that lay a solid foundation if you start with hearing each person's intention for participating. The following suggestions will help lay this foundation:

◆ Set an expectation that each person will get something out of the time spent together and that each will in turn give something to the group experience.

◆ Accept, acknowledge, and validate each person, including his or her hopes, concerns, resistance, and dreams, and you will begin to establish a community that includes everyone.

The first step you take establishes precedents and expectations for how the group will function. When people feel that they are being heard, they become engaged, willing, and motivated. When individuals see that their thinking is included, they begin to see themselves as part of a community. Connect what you will do to each person's interest, clarify the expectations of the principal or district, and show how they all fit together. Trust and safety are primary concerns when you get started, so start small and gradually construct a meaningful collective intention.

1. Offer choice about the degree to which any individual has to reveal vulnerability or doubt about his or her work.

2. Show by your actions that whatever is honest can be accepted and included in the discussion.

3. Explore options to accomplish this first step in 10 to 30 minutes (depending on how many people are in the group and how much time you allow for each person to talk).

4. Align individual goals with school and/or district goals.

BEGINNING ACTIVITY

Use simple, basic questions to prompt thinking and sharing about what people hope to achieve or receive through the group's work.

Ask two or three questions, such as those on the list below, for the whole group to discuss, or start with discussion in dyads before the whole-group discussion. If you have a particular curricular focus, such as math, or a specific population of students, you might want to add that focus at the end of any of the suggested questions.

You could pose only one question, ask one at a time, or pair two questions. Allow 30 to 60 seconds for people to think before sharing. You might also use a graphic organizer, with any of the questions, for people to use to reflect for a couple of minutes before sharing with the group.

Before you begin, think about how the questions could sound to members of the group. Dedicated teachers who worry they are never doing enough can be quick to hear implied criticism of their inadequacies, possibly leading to defensiveness. Validate the knowledge and success they already have. Talk about this as a chance to build on success, to get even better than they already are. Refer to specific successes you have seen.

Possible Questions

- Why are you here?
- What do you want to know more about?
- What do your students need?
- What do you want to do differently?
- What questions do you bring to this meeting?

Variations

1. My colleague Dave Schmid pairs complementary questions: one that he says comes from the heart and the other from the head. (adapted from Bob Chadwick)

    - How do you feel about being here today?
    - What are your expectations for this meeting?

2. If you have concerns that responses will be too negative, to hear balanced responses, ask:

    - What are your hopes for this meeting?
    - What are your concerns?
    - What are your wishes?

AIM: INSPIRATION

Be not simply good; be good for something.
— Henry David Thoreau

While a clear intention provides essential focus, if it does not inspire and touch our hearts, the potential power is limited. Children are a natural source of inspiration for teachers. By reading together excerpts from powerful texts, you provide a low-risk, indirect jumping-off point to inspire thoughts about children and place them at the center of the group's intention for what they will do.

CONSIDERATIONS

For teachers, focusing on students is familiar territory. That is our job, after all, so it would seem like a comfortable place to begin. However, if you move into an area that could reflect on a particular teacher's efficacy, it might not be so comfortable. While posing a question such as "What do we wish we could do for kids that we're not doing?" might jump-start your group to acknowledge there are places to improve, it could also be a risky and discouraging place to dive into without preparation. Teachers might feel that admitting to their students' gaps implies their own deficits, which may not be a good idea if you haven't yet established deep trust with one another. While a little risk is necessary in order to learn something new, it is best mixed with appropriate doses of safety and familiarity.

Reading short fiction can take us into the moments of a child's life and evoke memories of specific children and their vulnerabilities in ways that soften our hearts to do our work with and for them. You might ask each person to think of one child to hold in her mind through the discussion, a child he or she hopes will be impacted by the work this group is doing.

> ### Excerpt from
> ### "Salvador Late or Early"
>
> *Salvador with eyes the color of caterpillar, Salvador of the crooked hair and crooked teeth. Salvador whose name the teacher cannot remember, is a boy who is no one's friend, runs along somewhere in that vague direction where homes are the color of bad weather, lives behind a raw wood doorway, shakes the sleepy brothers awake, ties their shoes, combs their hair with water, feeds them milk and corn flakes from a tin cup in the dim dark of the morning.* (Cisneros, 1992)

There are many authors for children and young adults whose narratives lend themselves easily to the purpose of finding short, poignant excerpts. Some of the authors you may want to check out include Sandra Cisneros, Francisco Jiménez, Avi, Aliki, and Kevin Henkes (particularly for teachers of younger children).

By using a protocol to structure your discussion of the text, you can efficiently ensure focus and inclusion of each person's voice. Structure discussion of the text in groups of four or five in order to extract significant concepts within 25 minutes, for a total of about a half hour for the whole activity. Introduce the structure (see Fig. 5-1) before people read, so that while they read, they are aware they will be looking for a significant quote.

AIM: ENGAGEMENT

He who has a why to live for can bear almost any how.
— Friedrich Nietzsche

When people see potential personal value for themselves in achieving a goal, they are more likely to invest in it and commit to it with determination and focus.

As educators, we often have a hard time limiting what we expect of ourselves or are expected to give. Many of us are used to thinking we do everything "for the children." And

FIGURE 5-1: PROTOCOL

Text-Based Discussion: Save the Last Word for Me

PURPOSE: To deepen thinking about a text

YOU WILL NEED:

◆ Timekeeper/facilitator, who both participates and keeps the process moving

◆ Approximately 5 minutes for each round

◆ Groups of four or five participants

MATERIALS:

◆ Index cards

◆ A text

◆ A copy of the protocol for each participant

STEPS (Read through the steps before you begin.)

1. During or after reading, each person silently identifies a quote he or she considers most significant and writes the passage on one side of an index card, with notes on the reverse side about why it is significant.
   Directions to participants: The quote should resonate with you, perhaps stating an idea you agree or strongly disagree with.

2. When the group is ready, a volunteer reads aloud to the group his or her passage. This person (the presenter) says nothing about the quote at this point.
   Directions to participants: Identify where your quote appears in the text so that other members of the group can see it as well as hear it.

3. The other participants respond to the passage with their thoughts about why it is significant, what it makes them think about, questions it raises, and so on.
   Directions to participants: The format of this discussion could be either in round-robin style, with each person taking up to one minute, or an open discussion with an agreement to make sure everyone gets at least one chance to speak.

4. The person who selected the quote then has about two minutes to explain its significance. No one else comments. In other words, this person gets the last word.

5. The same pattern is repeated until everyone has had a chance to be the presenter and have "the last word."

6. Debrief the process with a prompt such as: How was this a useful format to explore the ideas in a text? Discuss implications for teaching.

Developed by Patricia Averette

Tools for Leaders © 2007 Marjorie Larner, Scholastic Professional

of course, we often believe that we never do enough. We are used to being what one colleague refers to as "martyrs for the cause."

To be fair, this is not just a personality fluke on our part. There is an expectation that educators choose teaching for purely altruistic reasons; indeed, the public sometimes voices suspicion toward teachers who advocate for salary increases, implying our devotion to students should transcend personal concerns. This is a heavy load to bear and perhaps one cause of burnout.

CONSIDERATIONS

Jeff Wein (a consultant for many schools and nonprofit educational organizations) often starts strategic planning meetings for faculty by asking people to identify what would be in it for them personally if the school or organization met its mission. He writes that "The key with this is to frame it so that teachers, administrators, etc. understand that in order to truly commit to a mission/vision, it is critical to take into account the interests of BOTH the client, i.e., students, and the professionals. However, in order to avoid using the clients as what I call a 'smokescreen' (e.g., 'Oh, I do this for the kids'), let's focus on the professionals' self interests without initially talking about the clients" (personal communication, 2006).

FIGURE 5-2: ACTIVITY

What's in It for Me?

PURPOSE: To provide an opportunity to think and talk about personal benefit in order to build genuine commitment to a mission or goal

STEPS

1. Post the goal of the group or school.

2. Post these two questions on chart paper, overhead or PowerPoint: Why is it in your individual and faculty self-interest to pursue this goal? What would you have to see/experience/receive on an ongoing basis in order to stay engaged in making it successful?

3. Allow time for participants to think and jot down notes in response to these two questions.

4. Direct participants to discuss these two questions (if the whole group has more than eight to ten members, break into small groups for this discussion, allowing time for these groups to share with the larger group highlights of their discussions).

5. Ask participants to brainstorm implications for their work together based on insights from this discussion.

Adapted from an activity developed by Jeff Wein

Tools for Leaders © 2007 Marjorie Larner, Scholastic Professional

---

Field Notes

I remember a group of social studies and athletics teachers who had to come to a breakout session I facilitated at a district in-service session before school started. They huddled in the back of the room. One pulled out a newspaper. Before we started, one of them said to me, "I hope you're not going to make us talk about *process*."

Well, that was, of course, the very thing we were going to talk about—processes for looking at student work that we hoped they would want to continue during the school year, with our help. They reminded me of high school students who didn't want to be in school. I knew I'd have to find a way to connect to their interests, validate their expertise, and leave room for them to make a connection to their teaching practice.

I suggested that there was a connection between what we were about to do in looking at some examples of student writing and what I believed they did as coaches. I asked them what they do when they watch athletes on the field, either in practice, in games, or on videos. They said they watch how the players move, what skills they use or need to strengthen, how they might be accommodating weaknesses. They look for small details that could be addressed to help their athletes increase their abilities on the field. I asked them to join us in looking at student work and bring that expertise in using student performance to inform teacher practice. They slowly rose from their chairs in the back of the room to join the group. And it was true. Each of these coaches brought an eye for detail, for describing what they saw and then for drawing implications about how to help the students with their work in the future.

CHAPTER 6
AGREEMENTS TO SUPPORT YOUR PURPOSE

My inner voice kept saying: "Talk to him. Talk to him. Don't just sit there."
—a fourth-grade student, reflecting on how he helped his friend in a writing conference

I once stepped into a land mine in front of a whole faculty when I asked the librarian how she scheduled classes through the day to ensure equitable time for everyone. After the gasps had died down and the principal changed the subject, I knew I had stumbled across one of their unspoken norms: never question the librarian. During the break, I asked a couple of teachers if they had established norms, and they told me, "Oh yeah. We have them in a book somewhere. Probably in the principal's office."

Over time in that school, I saw the norms they really used were powerful and unspoken. These were not the list in the notebook in the principal's office but rules internalized by everyone who had been in the building long enough to figure them out. They included a tacit agreement not to question one another's specific instructional practice, strong expectations for socializing, the weight that different people's opinions carried, the ways in which kids and their families could be talked about, and support for one another in times of stress.

Eventually I gathered the courage to lead a discussion to establish explicit agreements about how we needed to behave with one another to achieve the goals we had identified. This did not necessarily mean that no one was ever confronted or questioned. But it did mean that there were agreements about how and when it would be done.

A discussion that achieves consensus and establishes expectations for how group members will behave toward one another is a valuable practice in building trust and providing reassurance that, for the most part, people will behave in ways that allow us to hear each other and not hurt each other.

Norms often have a bad reputation with teachers because they have been handed to them, forced on them, developed in tedious wordsmithing meetings, and written in a notebook sitting somewhere on a shelf, with no input from the group about what they really want to commit to. So many times, when I hear about faculty having trouble working together, I ask them if they have established norms and they tell me, "Oh, yeah, we did that."

The bottom line is to come up with agreements that people will actually use to uphold standards that support productive work and promote ownership and commitment toward the group's functioning. Through discussion, the group creates collective meaning for the words on the list, invests the words with common meaning and understanding, and promotes ownership and commitment toward the group's productive functioning.

Explicit agreements become especially important if in the process of fulfilling your intentions and achieving your goals, you hit conflict or tensions. In those times, you might unconsciously fall into ways of treating one another that are not productive or safe. With established agreements, you can remind one another of commitments you have made as a group, without its being seen as a personal criticism.

Your goal may be not only to ensure that all group members are safe and comfortable, but also to make it possible for people to push themselves and one another to learn, grow, and change for the benefit of the school community.

AIM: CONSENSUS ON AGREEMENTS

I think it's important that all of us are aware of our own needs, but that we also stop to think if everyone is getting their needs met.
— first-grade teacher

While terms such as *norms*, *agreements*, and *ground rules* might be used interchangeably, depending on what feels best for a particular group, they carry subtly different meanings and expectations. So the first step is deciding on which term you will use.

♦ **Norms** are cultural agreements that are not necessarily created explicitly but nevertheless govern social behaviors.

♦ **Ground rules** are based on explicit agreements that guide the group's ability to work together effectively.

♦ **Operating agreements** are used in business as a contract that defines the roles and responsibilities and govern the business of an organization.

♦ **Community agreements** are traditionally developed by a group living together, though increasingly they are used in work communities to outline their vision and code of conduct to achieve that vision.

Whether you create norms, agreements, or ground rules, you might think of this process as creating a list of simple agreements about how you will treat one another. There are many ways to develop a list of agreements, but there are some essential components it should include:

♦ Shared understanding of the group's meaning and intent underlying each agreement

- Genuine commitment to following agreements
- Explicit ownership residing in the group
- Expectation for revision as a document in progress

GUIDELINES FOR FACILITATION OF THE DISCUSSION

- Keep a steady pace toward a list of no more than four or five agreements. Set a time limit on the discussion to prevent endless debates. If you can't come to agreement, leave it as an open question to be revisited. Ask the group: Can you live with this ambiguity for now?
- Encourage people to talk about agreements in terms of behaviors rather than concepts. They will often start by saying things like "respect each other" or "build trust." Push them to say what it would look like to respect each other, and ask what they do to respect one another. Other evocative questions might include these: What is the behavior that leads you to feel and show respect? What does trust look like to you?
- Bring up concrete aspects of your group's functioning. Ask people to think about what they will do when conflicts arise, how they will arrive at decisions, how they will ensure everyone has a say. Pose questions such as: How will decisions be made? How will conflicts be addressed?
- Ask people to think about not only what works for them but what will be in the best interest of the group to fulfill their intentions.

WORK FROM EXAMPLES

Provide a list of agreements for the group to work from, so they don't have to reinvent the wheel. This list can be used to start a discussion focused on what is needed and not needed for this particular group to work together. (See Fig. 6-1 for a structure to discuss agreement.) Through the discussion, everyone will learn more about one another and construct collective meaning and understanding of what the group needs in order to fulfill its intentions.

Following is a compilation of agreements from different schools to help you come up with your own list to present to get your group discussion started. You could choose four or five from this list, or perhaps they will spark ideas of your own.

Sample Agreements

- Watch (share) airtime.
- Listen for understanding.
- Listen and be open.
- Maintain confidentiality.
- Presume positive intention.
- Support one another's learning.
- Take responsibility for your own learning.
- If you wonder, ask . . .
- Participate.
- Be truthful and speak up.
- Be fully present.
- Ensure everyone shares responsibility for the group.
- Have fun.
- Give gentle reminders.

FIGURE 6-1: PROTOCOL

Establishing Agreements

PURPOSE: Develop consensus and collective understandings regarding group behavior

TIME: Approximately 20–30 minutes

STEPS

1. The group discusses what these agreements mean to them: What is most important? What will be most challenging? With more than eight to ten people, break into dyads or smaller groups of three or four for this discussion, with reporting back to whole group.

2. The group offers suggestions for rewording or revising, adding or omitting.

3. Ask if everyone can commit to this list. How will we help one another adhere to agreements once they are established?

4. Each person identifies and writes down one agreement that could be personally challenging that he or she will work on maintaining.

5. Volunteers share the agreement they have chosen.

Tools for Leaders © 2007 Marjorie Larner, Scholastic Professional

AIM: KEEP AGREEMENTS CURRENT

Agreements are most useful, and most used, when they are held as a living document that is revisited and revised as the group continues to learn and grow. As you develop trust in your community, you may find that the group needs new agreements to support the developing level of risk in conversations. Or, the same words can take on new meaning as group members move into previously avoided topics of conversation. Eventually, group members may question some agreements that don't serve everyone equally well. Revisiting agreements on a regular basis can be a vital opportunity to gain insights into cultural and personal differences that influence each person's experience. Within the following three simple questions are the roots for your group interactions at every stage of your developing capacity to work and learn together.

◆ Are the agreements working to ensure the group's safety and productivity?

◆ How are we doing as a group in sticking to the agreements?

◆ How are we doing as individuals?

AIM: ARTICULATE CORE BELIEFS

They were so strong in their beliefs that there came a time when it hardly mattered what exactly those beliefs were; they all fused into a single stubbornness.
— Louise Erdrich

It is our beliefs that fuel and sustain our commitments and are often at the root of the failure to come to consensus on agreements or other important elements of collaboration. When we are clear about our beliefs, we create a larger context for our commitment.

CONSIDERATIONS

As you have probably seen firsthand, two people can argue forever about beliefs and get nowhere. This is in part due to the nature of beliefs, which are not necessarily based on evidence but rather on interpretations of experience. Accepting that you will probably not change another person's beliefs, you can decide if it is going to be possible to move forward allowing for differences, or if the beliefs are so crucial to practice that you need to push through to find common ground for the sake of the school. By providing an opportunity for people to think about their own beliefs, articulate them, and listen to others' beliefs, you establish more understanding and awareness to bring to discussions, particularly when conflicts arise.

To begin a discussion about the beliefs held by the group, read these excerpts (Fig. 6-2) from the chapter "Beyond Technique" in Ron Ritchhart's book *Intellectual Character: What It Is, Why It Matters, and How to Get It,* followed by either an informal or formal discussion. Listen to one another for shared beliefs as well as disagreements. See if and where consensus naturally occurs. Remember that consensus does not mean that everyone agrees but that those who still disagree, even after a discussion, are willing to go along and see what happens.

ACTIVITIES TO IDENTIFY RED THREADS

Often we are not aware of our most deeply held beliefs, though they are what determine our actions and behaviors. To help each person identify his or her red thread, you might start a conversation by talking about your own recurring themes and then ask others to share theirs.

Joy Hood developed a list of prompts (bottom of Fig. 6-3) to provide structure for teachers to identify their core beliefs and the actions that follow from those beliefs. You can use this for a brief discussion to get beliefs out in the open, where you can acknowledge their part in the dynamics of your discussion. You can also take more time to go deeper into participants' beliefs (see Fig. 6-4 and 6-5) and how they impact everyone's practice and work.

FIGURE 6-2: READING

Exploring Foundations

The foundations of a teacher's practice, the way he or she makes decisions and manages dilemmas, can't be uncovered by looking at its outward manifestations. Nor can its source be discerned by merely aggregating some combination of experience and training. To get to the root of teaching, we have to look inside the teacher at the various values, beliefs, theories, and knowledge that person holds: values about what is important to teach; theories of instruction; and knowledge about the subject matter, curriculum, and pedagogical practices. Uncovering these roots isn't always easy. Beliefs, values, and implicit theories can be elusive things, difficult for both the researcher and the teacher to grab hold of and hang on to. Furthermore, it isn't always clear what information we can consider reliable and trustworthy. How do we know when we have tapped into core beliefs? How do we know when these elements are affecting a teacher's practice? (181–182)

The Red Thread

The red thread is used in a variety of cultures as a metaphor for connecting, binding, and uniting. I was first introduced to it by Swedish colleagues who used the expression in the context of finding a central commonality across different situations. In Hebrew, the word *theme* translates literally as "the red thread." In Chinese culture, the red thread represents the invisible connections that bind every newborn to all of the important people in that child's life. In Buddhism, the red thread signifies passion. Thus, I feel the red thread is an apt metaphor for describing beliefs, passions, values, and goals that tie together and unite a teacher's practice over time and contexts. The red thread doesn't represent a single belief, however, but a set of deeply held beliefs. Thus, I was not looking to find a single core value or belief but a core collection that would aptly capture each teacher's agenda. . . .

To unearth teachers' red threads, I interviewed them about their goals, values, and beliefs, and I observed their classrooms in order to uncover the implicit messages in their instruction. I analyzed the interviews for recurring themes that appeared in both the interviews and the teacher's instruction. This ensures that the theme is not just a philosophical stance the teacher took during the interview but one that the teacher's practice embodies. (Ritchhart, 2002)

FIGURE 6-3: ACTIVITY

Belief Activity

DIRECTIONS TO PARTICIPANTS

1. Complete the sentence stems below. Add words that relate to your specific situation, such as "I believe learning. . . ." (10 minutes)

2. Share beliefs in dyads, triads, or small groups. (5–10 minutes)

3. Discuss beliefs. Look for individual and group recurring themes—can you articulate a few shared core beliefs from this list? (5–10 minutes)

4. Share with whole group. Discuss implications, patterns, agreements, and disagreements. (20–30 minutes)

FURTHER STEPS

1. Discuss teaching actions that fit with your beliefs and those that don't fit with your beliefs. Look at the impact and implications of what you discover.

2. Identify common core beliefs and their influence on the collaborative work of your group or team. How do these beliefs fit within the work you have set for yourselves?

3. Work toward consensus for a set of core beliefs held by the whole faculty. Identify actions that follow on these beliefs: We believe _____ and so we _____. An additional organizer is included for people to record their thoughts (Fig. 6–4).

I Believe . . .

I believe children . . .

I believe teachers . . .

I believe teaching . . .

I believe education . . .

I believe parents . . .

I believe schools . . .

I believe learning . . .

I believe I . . .

I believe our school . . .

Tools for Leaders © 2007 Marjorie Larner, Scholastic Professional

FIGURE 6-4: ORGANIZER

BELIEF ORGANIZER

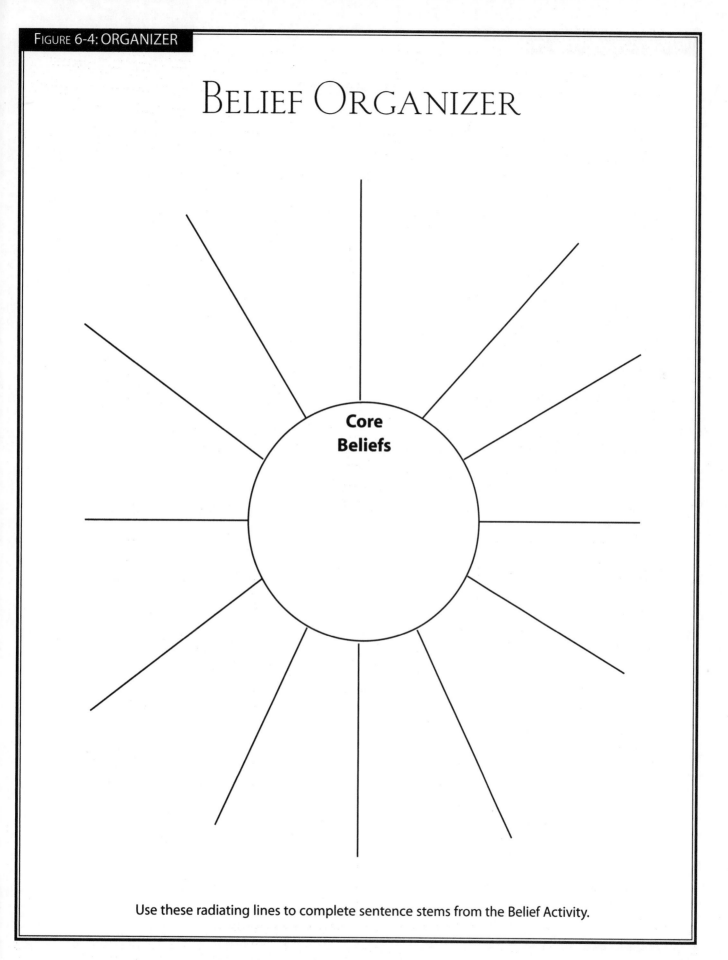

Core Beliefs

Use these radiating lines to complete sentence stems from the Belief Activity.

FIGURE 6-5: ACTIVITY

Web Activity

PURPOSE: To provide an opportunity for each person in a group to share a brief thought with a visual picture of the interconnectedness of all the individuals. Depending on your context, you could ask each person to share a belief, a feeling at the end of a meeting, an idea for action, and so on.

MATERIALS:
- Ball of yarn or string (needs to be heavy enough to throw)
- Scissors

STEPS

1. Stand in a circle.

2. Tell the group that everyone will have a turn to share a brief thought.

3. Hand the ball of yarn or string to a person who will go first.

4. The first person shares a brief thought.

5. After sharing her belief, she holds on to one end of the string and tosses the ball to another person who catches it and shares her thought.

6. Continue until everyone has had a chance to share.

7. Ask everyone to lay the string on the floor and let go. Give everyone a minute or so to admire the web of your connections with each other.

8. Cut off a piece of the string for each person to take (tape in notebook, wear on wrist until it falls off, and so on) as a visual reminder of the support and strength of the group.

Tools for Leaders © 2007 Marjorie Larner, Scholastic Professional

FIELD NOTES

At the beginning of the school year, elementary teacher Carrie Symons talks with her students about the concept of the red thread and how it influences our choices about what we do. Over the next few days, they have discussions about their beliefs. She provides sentence stems for them to complete that are relevant to their current experience, such as homework, studying, friends. They discuss how they will behave as the result of their beliefs. When someone does something particularly noteworthy, they talk about how the action matches a belief shared by the classroom community. She gives each student a piece of red thread to tape into a notebook or wear around the wrist. In her classroom, the red thread bracelet helps the students develop their identity as members of a community.

Chapter 7
Listening to Each Other

Education is a kind of continuing dialogue, and a dialogue assumes, in the nature of the case, different points of view.
— Robert Hutchins

As the conversation in my work with the National School Reform Faculty has moved more deeply into issues of equity, in keeping with our mission to foster educational and social equity, the points of view have become more passionate and divergent. We are going into new territory. I am hearing things from other people about their experiences with racism, oppression, and bias that I don't want to accept as true. It has been hard to hold my own tongue and listen when I hear things that touch my nerves and contradict my own opinions and experiences. In the thick of it, our agreements and structures have allowed me to listen without outwardly reacting, to take in what is being said, and finally, to understand points of view that have expanded my understanding and capacity as a teacher. With each opportunity to practice and experience the value of listening, it becomes slightly easier to listen well the next time.

I have also seen that there is a direct connection between how teachers work with one another and how they work with students. Working with colleagues who represent different perspectives and backgrounds increases knowledge and capacity to work with students who come from different perspectives and backgrounds.

Traditionally in our culture, when people don't completely agree, they fall into a debate until one person is ready to give up, so only one point of view prevails. In a way, that defeats the whole purpose of bringing individuals together. If you only wanted one point of view, you could just let one person tell everyone what to do.

It takes time and practice to change this habit of debate and the holding of one position. It takes a willingness to try out something foreign. Here is a story I've heard repeated over the years about Fritz Perls, a highly respected Gestalt therapist, when he was confronted by two members of opposing factions in a conflict that was raging at Esalen, the infamous California New Age health retreat. After listening to a spokesman for one side give his heartfelt argument, Perls stood silent for a moment, then said, "Well . . . you're right."

The spokesman for the opposite view then stepped forward. "But wait a minute. You haven't heard our side."

And so, Perls listened to another explanation. After the man was finished explaining, Perls said, "Well . . . you're right."

A student of Perls who had been listening stepped forward and questioned what he had just heard. "Fritz, do you know what you just did? You just agreed with two diametrically opposed ideas."

Perls looked thoughtfully at this man and replied:

"Well . . . you're right."

AIM: DEVELOPING HABITS OF LISTENING

We are what we repeatedly do. Excellence, therefore, is not an act but a habit.
— Aristotle

In a typical meeting, some voices are heard over others. Certain opinions and points of view gather power, while dissenting or minority points of view diminish. Typical meetings work best for those of us who are naturally adept at jumping into conversations and insisting we have our turn to talk. In fact, people who are verbal processors may take a lot of everyone's time as they dominate the airspace, thinking aloud and taking the discussion in a direction they want it to go until someone else finds a way to jump in for their turn.

If you like to think for a while before you speak or are not aggressive enough to jump in fast, if you are uncertain about your right to a position, you may find that by the time you are ready and willing to speak, the conversation has moved on to something else, often a tangent of the intended topic. Or you may notice and worry about other people's silence as an indication of their disengagement, disconnection, or judgment.

Many of us are used to this experience and perhaps that is why so many people do not look forward to going to meetings.

Structures and routines can guide you and your group as you refine and develop habits for participating in a community where everyone shares responsibility for the productive, respectful, stimulating environment you create together.

CONSIDERATIONS

You might say that speaking and listening are two sides of the same coin. Like the sound of the tree falling in the forest, talk without anyone to hear it (even if it is just listening to your own inner dialogue) is impossible to imagine. Furthermore, have you noticed how a good listener can make a good speaker out of almost anyone? Think of a time when you were engaged in a conversation with a colleague and knew she wasn't really interested in your talk, and contrast it with a time you felt you were being heard and understood. As teachers, we have many opportunities to experience these different scenarios.

The key to this process is developing your habits of both listening to and expressing different points of view so that the potential view of the whole group is much bigger than the sum of its parts. You will also become more conscious of words that contribute to another person's thinking, that solve problems, and that help move the group forward.

AIM: PRACTICING A NEW KIND OF LISTENING

It will take a special kind of listening, listening that requires not only open eyes and ears, but open hearts and minds. . . . It is not easy, but it is the only way to learn what it might feel like to be someone else and the only way to start the dialogue.

— Lisa Delpit

Constructivist listening is a skill you will find useful as a coach, administrator, and teacher. It also has a place in most protocols, whether you are a facilitator, presenter, or participant. When you practice constructivist listening, you become more aware of your automatic reactions, which increases your capacity to offer targeted, useful responses.

CONSIDERATIONS

With the consistent structures that protocols provide, most people begin to form habits of listening and speaking up, wanting to hear from everyone, noticing when they slide off on tangents, or talk too much or too little. They may even begin to carry these habits into other interactions with children and adults. When these patterns of working together are established, we can achieve what Adlai Stevenson envisioned as a free society "where it is safe to be unpopular."

The following activity to practice constructivist listening (Fig. 7-1) is useful in many contexts—before, during, or after a structured discussion—as it allows each person a chance for expression with a good listener. You could spend a few minutes in dyads using constructivist listening at the beginning of a meeting to help people get started thinking, during a heated discussion crowded with passionate opinions, or after a discussion to reflect and synthesize.

FIGURE 7-1: ACTIVITY

Constructivist Listening Dyad

PURPOSE: To create a safe space in which to become better at listening and talking in depth

INTRODUCTION: Constructivist listening dyads help us as we work through feelings, thoughts, and beliefs that sometimes produce anger or passivity, undermine confidence, or interfere in relationships with students or colleagues. Each person has an opportunity to think aloud with a receptive listener who is there for the benefit of the speaker.

TIME: 20–30 minutes

MATERIALS: A timer

FACILITATION TIPS: Talk about the purpose of a constructivist listening dyad.

Explain to participants that the simplest form of doing constructivist listening is a dyad, which is the exchange of constructivist listening between two people who make this commitment: "I agree to listen to and think about you for a fixed period of time in exchange for your doing the same for me. I keep in mind that my listening is for your benefit so I do not ask questions for my information."

Start with each person talking for two minutes—at first it may seem difficult. But over the course of time, participants may work their way up to five to eight minutes and more each.

Remind participants that in a constructivist listening dyad, the listening is for the benefit of the talker. This is an essential point so the speaker will not be worrying about what the listener is hearing but rather, in effect, the speaker hears his own inner thoughts spoken aloud.

GUIDELINES FOR CONSTRUCTIVIST LISTENING:

- Each person is given equal time to talk. (Everyone deserves to be listened to.)
- The listener does not interpret, paraphrase, analyze, give advice, or break in with a personal story. (People can solve their own problems.)
- Confidentiality is maintained. (People need to know they can be completely authentic.)
- The talker does not criticize or complain about the listener or about mutual colleagues during their time to talk. (A person cannot listen well when he or she is feeling attacked or defensive.)

STEPS

1. Each person will have two minutes or more to respond to a prompt. It is very useful to scaffold the prompts. **Example:** When is the last time you remember being fully listened too? How did it feel?
   - Growing up, what was your experience as a learner? What felt supportive? What interfered with your learning?
   - How did race, class, or gender impact your experience as a learner in school?

2. Reflection (debrief) questions following the activity:
   - What came up for you using this structure? What came up for you reflecting on the prompt?
   - What worked for you? What was difficult for you?
   - What purpose do you think it might serve?

Adapted from the work of Victor Cary, National Coalition for Equity in Education (www.nsrfharmony.org)

Tools for Leaders © 2007 Marjorie Larner, Scholastic Professional

Aim: Reading to Consider New Ways

To start a discussion and shift ideas about listening, the following short texts, which can be read silently or aloud in a few minutes, bring in powerful new perspectives. (See Fig. 7-4 and 7-5.)

Following the reading, take a few minutes for people to share their reactions or use one of the protocols, such as Text-Based Discussion: Save the Last Word for Me (Chapter 5), Text Rendering (Fig. 7-2), or Text-Based Seminar (Fig. 7-3). If you use a protocol, distribute copies so everyone can share responsibility for adhering to the steps in the process.

FIGURE 7-2: PROTOCOL

Text Rendering

PURPOSE: To collaboratively construct meaning, clarify and expand our thinking about a text or document

ROLES:
- ◆ A facilitator to guide the process
- ◆ Two scribes to chart the words that are shared (with two scribes, you don't have to wait after each person for the word to be written, so the words are heard with an even flow, like a poem)

STEPS (Read through the steps before you begin.)
Ask participants to take a few minutes to read or review the document and mark the sentence, the phrase, and the word that catches their attention, stands out for them, and seems important to their work.

1. First round: Each person shares a sentence that he or she feels is particularly significant.

2. Second round: Each person shares a phrase that he or she feels is particularly significant.

3. Third round: Each person shares the word that he or she feels is particularly significant. The scribes alternate recording each word on chart paper visible to everyone.

4. The group discusses new insights about the document.

5. Debrief the process.

Option: With a large group, break into smaller groups for steps 1–4, then come back together as a whole group and repeat steps 3–4.

Developed in the field by educators affiliated with the NSRF (www.nsrfharmony.org)

Tools for Leaders © 2007 Marjorie Larner, Scholastic Professional

---

Figure 7-3: Protocol

Text-Based Seminar

Purpose: To build a common understanding of a text; to deepen one's understanding of a text (text is defined broadly: an article, a book, a video, an art presentation, etc.)

Steps (Read through the steps before you begin.)

1. Facilitator selects a text and frames a question or two that will shape the discussion.

2. Group reads the text like a love letter: over and over to nudge meaning out of every word.

3. Facilitator opens the discussion with these reminders to the group:
   - Stay focused on the framing question.
   - Ground comments to a specific place in the text.
   - Challenge ideas with respect for divergent points of view.
   - Share responsibility for the success of the discussion.

4. Debrief the process.

Developed by Gene Thompson-Grove

Tools for Leaders © 2007 Marjorie Larner, Scholastic Professional

HABITS OF LISTENING

Listen! Or your tongue will make you deaf. — Cherokee saying

The whole group suffers if you don't hear from everyone. In the traditional Iroquois council, there is a rule that everyone waits a few minutes after a person finishes speaking to make sure he has completed all he has to say. The deep belief is that we all profit from hearing each other, at least as much as from hearing ourselves.

We are so accustomed to our ways of interacting that it can be challenging to even imagine how it could be different. To offer another picture of how people can interact around serious issues, read and discuss this description of rules and customs established for the legendary Iroquois Great Council (Fig. 7-4) that brought together seven nations that had previously been at war with one another.

While you read and discuss this excerpt from Jean Houston's *Manual of the Peacemaker*, think about how this approach could translate and bring benefit to your meetings. How might you start your meetings with thankfulness for what is going well, acknowledgment of each voice in the room, and consideration of ideas from multiple perspectives?

FIGURE 7-4: READING

The Great Tree of Peace

Deganawidah [also] provided the nation with a pattern for meetings of the yearly Great Council. Each opened with a prayer of thanksgiving to the earth and to all that was in it: "I thank you for the earth. I thank you for the waters. I thank you for the corn and for the harvest." Thanks were also given to a prodigious number of particular things that it seemed nothing could have been left out. This tradition is a magnificent teaching: discussions and problems can be considered only after everyone is in an exhilarated state of thanksgiving! And not even then, for next came songs to commemorate the founding of the League. Then came a kind of choral roll call of the tribes, with each acknowledging its attendance by song or chant. After all this, when they sat before the council fire, proposals were made with the use of wampum, and three kinds of debate were held for each issue: within a tribe, with a sister tribe, and then with the entire confederacy. In our terms, it would be like debating an issue within one's state, within one's bioregion, and then nationally. If discussion became stymied because of insoluble disagreements, the issue was sent back to the point in the process at which the debate had foundered. The Onondaga representative, as keeper of the fire, could break a tie vote or make a choice when two sides failed.

In another wise decision, Deganawidah declared that the Great Council was to be adjourned when night fell, because overlong discussions might lead to raised tempers and thus become a threat to peace. Council debates knew no such thing as filibustering. An issue was not open to public debate on the day it was put before the council. Instead, everybody thought about an issue for a while after it was presented, and only then did they bring it up for discussion.

Another cherished tradition encouraged by Deganawidah and practiced by many tribes in the Americas was the use of the wampum strands as an aid to serious talking and deep listening. It was understood that when a speaker in council held the wampum, he or she would speak from his or her deepest truth and most essential knowing. By tradition, others weren't allowed to jump up to make their points. Instead, they were to attend fully to what was being said as the belt of wampum passed from speaker to speaker. "Deepen the issue" was the spoken and unspoken guidance. Imagine how it would be if the presiding officer of the Senate were to say, "Will the Junior Senator from Vermont please rise and deepen the issue that the Senior Senator from Minnesota has raised?"

Benjamin Franklin, who observed at first hand the workings of the Haundenosaunee government, had this to say about the conduct of council meetings: "He that would speak, rises. The rest observe a profound Silence. When he has finished and sits down, they leave him five or six minutes to recollect, that he has omitted anything he intended to say, or has anything to add, he may rise again and deliver it. To interrupt another, even in common Conversation, is reckoned highly indecent. How different it is from the conduct of a polite British House of Commons, where scarce a Day passes without some Confusion that makes the Speaker hoarse in calling to order and how different from the mode of Conversation in many polite Companies of Europe, where if you do not deliver your Sentence with great Rapidity, you are cut off in the middle of it by the impatient Loquacity of those you converse with & never suffer'd to finish it." (Houston, 1995)

Tools for Leaders © 2007 Marjorie Larner, Scholastic Professional

LISTENING WHEN YOU DISAGREE

You don't get harmony when everybody sings the same note. — Doug Floyd

Once, while I was working with a group looking at an intractable achievement gap between English language learners and native English speakers at the high school level, one of the teachers stated that his focus in joining this group was to help his immigrant students assimilate into the mainstream culture, as his ancestors had done, even if it meant letting go of their native languages, idioms, styles, and habits. This was a very unpopular position, with several other teachers holding a core belief that immigrants should be supported to hold onto their native language, culture, and identity.

Because we had slowed down the dialogue, allowing everyone a chance to speak and providing some space between comments, the teachers who otherwise might have

---

To Teachers

There are many benefits to slowing down, allowing people to have their say, considering listening as much an active participation as talking. When people know they will have their chance to speak, they are often more able to listen and consider another person's point of view. When people are ensured an opening into a conversation, they are often more able to fully articulate their thoughts.

I have had to acknowledge that there were times I was one of those domineering people, and perhaps that is why I am so sympathetic to their concern. I have also been silenced in a group and know the results of that. Think about what roles you take in a group discussion. If you push yourself to try the option that is not comfortable for you (listening or talking), you are likely to find exciting new avenues for experience and participation open up for you.

---

jumped into the discussion and on his comment, if not him, had time to take a breath, gather their thoughts, and speak in a way that invited dialogue rather than merely shutting him off. He heard a point of view he hadn't heard clearly articulated before.

These positions, and there were more than two, needed to be brought out into the open because they impacted participation and the potential outcome for the project. While no one substantially changed his or her position at that moment, there was an opportunity to share experiences and learning from different sides of a touchy and complex issue.

The group revisited and revised their focus from a broad "how to narrow the achievement gap" to "take a look with new eyes at student experiences in classrooms in order to better understand how to guide them on paths to learning and achievement in their public school." One consequence of pushing each other's assumptions was that it established a

Troubleshooting: Talking Through Dissonance

Doubt is not a pleasant condition, but certainty is absurd. — Voltaire

When a person in a group doesn't agree with the majority viewpoint, and he or she can't find a way to influence the discussion but instead feels pressure to give in and conform, the next step may be withdrawal, either verbally, mentally, or even physically. You can't always prevent this from happening, but you can make sure you give time in the group, and in private if necessary, for the person to be not just heard but really considered. Minority opinions, individual dissonant voices, often express what no one else has the nerve to bring to the table, because they don't want to make people uncomfortable. It is precisely this discomfort, which usually signals something needs to be taken into account, that can lead to greater learning.

When people are locked in a debate and making no progress hearing one another, see if they will take the other side as an exercise to stretch their minds. You might have to inject a little humor to get people to be willing to step aside from the tension developed over the conflict. Ask each person to state the opposing position "as if it were your own." Argue the other side by imagining the beliefs, convictions, and consequences that are part of this point of view. Debrief what it felt like to hold that position by asking, "What do you understand about it now?"

Another way to break the dynamic of opposition is to ask people to look at the assumptions underlying their position and then discuss those assumptions first. For instance, the dissenter in this story acknowledged his assumption that being part of the mainstream culture is a primary value. The other position assumed that there is great loss for a person who lets go of his culture of origin. They found they shared the view that everyone who comes to this country is entitled to success in school.

precedent for honest, tough conversations. Not only was there more conversation among the teachers, but there was more talk and collaboration between students and teachers.

To get across the idea that there is value for each of us in hearing opposing ideas, the excerpt (Fig. 7-5) from Margaret Wheatley's book, *Turning to One Another,* provides a beautifully written argument for changing our way of listening.

FIGURE 7-5: READING

Willing to Be Disturbed

As we work together to restore hope to the future, we need to include a new and strange ally—our willingness to be disturbed, our willingness to have our beliefs and ideas challenged by what others think. No one person or perspective can give us the answers we need to the problems of today. Paradoxically, we can only find those answers by admitting we don't know. We have to be willing to let go of our certainty and expect ourselves to be confused for a time.

We weren't trained to admit we don't know. Most of us were taught to sound certain and confident, to state our opinion as if it were true. We haven't been rewarded for being confused. Or for asking more questions rather than giving quick answers. We've also spent many years listening to others mainly to determine whether we agree with them or not. We don't have time or interest to sit and listen to those who think differently than we do.

But the world now is quite perplexing. We no longer live in those sweet, slow days when life felt predictable, when we actually knew what to do next. We live in a complex world, we often don't know what's going on, and we won't be able to understand its complexity unless we spend more time in not knowing.

It is very difficult to give up our certainties—our positions, our beliefs, our explanations. These help define us; they lie at the heart of our personal identity. Yet I believe we will succeed in changing this world only if we can think and work together in new ways. Curiosity is what we need. We don't have to let go of what we believe, but we do need to be curious about what someone else believes. We do need to acknowledge that their way of interpreting the world might be essential to our survival.

We live in a dense and tangled global system. Because we live in different parts of this complexity, and because no two people are physically identical, we each experience life differently. It's impossible for any two people to ever see things exactly the same. You can test this out for yourself. Take any event that you've shared with others (a speech, a movie, a current event, a major problem) and ask your colleagues and friends to describe their interpretation of that event. I think you'll be amazed at how many different explanations you'll hear. Once you get a sense of the diversity, try asking even more colleagues. You'll end up with a rich tapestry of interpretations that are much more interesting than any single one.

To be curious about how someone else interprets things, we have to be willing to admit that we're not capable of figuring things out alone. If our solutions don't work as well as we want them to, if our explanations of why something happened don't feel sufficient, it's time to begin asking others about what they see and think. When so many interpretations are available, I can't understand why we would be satisfied with superficial conversations where we pretend to agree with one another.

There are many ways to sit and listen for the differences. Lately, I've been listening for what surprises me. What did I just hear that startled me? This isn't easy—I'm accustomed to sitting

FIGURE 7-5, PAGE 2

there nodding my head to those saying things I agree with. But when I notice what surprises me, I'm able to see my own views more clearly, including my beliefs and assumptions.

Noticing what surprises and disturbs me has been a very useful way to see invisible beliefs. If what you say surprises me, I must have been assuming something else was true. If what you say disturbs me. I must believe something contrary to you. My shock at your position exposes my own position. When I hear myself saying, "How could anyone believe something like that?" a light comes on for me to see my own beliefs. These moments are great gifts. If I can see my beliefs and assumptions, I can decide whether I still value them.

I hope you'll begin a conversation, listening for what's new. Listen as best you can for what's different, for what surprises you. See if this practice helps you learn something new. Notice whether you develop a better relationship with the person you're talking with. If you try this with several people, you might find yourself laughing in delight as you realize how many unique ways there are to be human.

We have the opportunity many times a day, every day, to be the one who listens to others, curious rather than certain. But the greatest benefit of all is that listening moves us closer. When we listen with less judgment, we always develop better relationships with each other. It's not differences that divide us. It's our judgments about each other that do. Curiosity and good listening bring us back together.

Sometimes we hesitate to listen for differences because we don't want to change. We're comfortable with our lives, and if we listened to anyone who raised questions, we'd have to get engaged in changing things. If we don't listen, things can stay as they are and we won't have to expend any energy. But most of us do see things in our life or in the world that we would like to be different. If that's true, we have to listen more, not less. And we have to be willing to move into the very uncomfortable place of uncertainty.

We can't be creative if we refuse to be confused. Change always starts with confusion; cherished interpretations must dissolve to make way for the new. Of course it's scary to give up what we know, but the abyss is where newness lives. Great ideas and inventions miraculously appear in the space of not knowing. If we can move through the fear and enter the abyss, we are rewarded greatly. We rediscover we're creative.

As the world grows more strange and puzzling and difficult, I don't believe most of us want to keep struggling through it alone. I can't know what to do from my own narrow perspective. I know I need a better understanding of what's going on. I want to sit down with you and talk about all the frightening and hopeful things I observe, and listen to what frightens you and gives you hope. I need new ideas and solutions for the problems I care about. I know I need to talk to you to discover those. I need to learn to value your perspective, and I want you to value mine. I expect to be disturbed by what I hear from you. I know we don't have to agree with each other in order to think well together. There is no need for us to be joined at the head. We are joined by our human hearts. (Wheatley, 2002, pp. 34–37)

FIELD NOTES

Education is the ability to listen to almost anything without losing your temper or your self-confidence.
— Robert Frost

With current statistics about low graduation rates in urban high schools and the disparity in outcomes for different populations of students, I have seen more willingness to address the questions of equity head on. This is a complex and thorny endeavor, with dissonance and discomfort, that takes commitment to push through. The quotes below provide a pathway to follow.

The first two quotes work as preludes to constructivist listening dyads (Fig. 7-1) using the questions related to our own stories of inequity/equity. I use one of the text discussion protocols (Figs. 5-1, 7-2, 7-3) with the last two quotes as a means of leading into planning for action.

There are many ways to do diversity work. The most exciting, the most effective entry point as I see it, is helping people learn how to talk and listen to one another. Everyone has a story to tell about the impact of differences on their lives and careers. Most people want to tell their story. The heart and soul of this work is giving people the chance to talk. — Barbara Walker

Groups can often avoid unproductive situations if members recognize that inequity and prejudice have grown out of societal oppression or distressing earlier experiences. People need opportunities to work through the feelings from these hurts. Participants also need to be reminded that emotional release (through tears, trembling, laughing, and talking, for example) is the natural healing process from the distress they have experienced. It is also important for people to be able to talk about the first time they encountered prejudice and inequity, and their feelings at the time. — Julian Weissglass, director of the Equity in Mathematics Education Leadership Institute

We agree with Mr. Weissglass's concise diagnosis, but he does not go deeply enough into the structures and policies that allow racism to be active in the lives of children and the business of our schools. We have to change the facts, not just the feelings that nurture and are nurtured by deep and historic social engineering that divides races and economic classes in America. It will take honest dialogue and leadership, but also much more than that to put our society and our students on equitable footing. — National Urban Alliance for Effective Education

Let's ask ourselves the question: "Am I courageous enough to propose to another, who I have differences with, a crazy theory of working together that would bring our collective imaginations into focus?"
— adapted from the Iowa Peace Institute

Chapter 8
Working Relationships

Discovery consists in seeing what everyone else has seen but understanding it for the first time.
— Albert Szent-Gyorgyi

A few years ago, I worked with a group of coaches in Cleveland who kept telling us they wanted to do more team-building activities. They had a hard time convincing us that was a worthwhile use of our limited once-a-month seminars. Theress Pidick, my partner, and I agreed that team building was not only fluff but out of date, given the seriousness of current times. But we noticed our colleagues out in the hallways with their groups, who were pretty lively, laughing, crying, very engaged. We began to wonder if they knew something we didn't know and concluded that they did.

We listened to our group and asked for volunteers to lead team-building activities at our meetings. With these activities, the group dynamic changed. The more we learned about one another, the more genuinely interested, patient, and concerned we were. I realized I actually loved these activities that provided a chance to learn with our bodies and hearts as well as our minds. Through them, we created a foundation for doing real work, facing our hard challenges, growing in our capacity as coaches. Framed in a way to clearly relate to the issues and dilemmas faced by participants, team-building activities provided a base from which to address those dilemmas together.

Aim: Building Relationships

Activities such as the four that follow (Fig. 8-1 through 8-4) provide a chance for people to see beyond assumptions based on the limits of how we normally know or see one another. They also serve as energizers, particularly after coming back from lunch or meeting, when people are sluggish and need a chance to get out of their chair.

CONSIDERATIONS

Even with structures and agreements, the capacity for listening and speaking up is impacted by views and feelings about the people with whom you are meeting. Whenever a group is forming, even if individuals have already "done the activity" in another context, think about using it again so this new group can get to know about each other. Even in a group that has worked together before, people change, and there is always more to learn about one another.

FIGURE 8-1: ACTIVITY

Crumpled Confessions

PURPOSE: To get to know each other beyond the usual professional relationships; to crack open assumptions about how we see each other

STEPS

1. Distribute a slip of paper to each participant.
    Facilitator provides a prompt such as these:
    - ◆ Describe something wild you did in college.
    - ◆ Describe a time you got in trouble (as a child).
    - ◆ What is something we wouldn't know just by looking at you?

2. Each participant writes his or her brief story on a piece of paper and then crumples it up.

3. Participants stand in a circle and toss crumpled papers into the center.

4. First person selects a paper and reads it aloud, makes a guess about whom it belongs to, and hands the paper to that person, who holds onto it without saying anything. Then that person takes a turn.

5. This continues until everyone has taken a turn reading and guessing. If someone who has already taken a turn is handed a paper, then a person nearby who has not had a turn goes next. One person may be handed more than one slip of paper.

6. After everyone has taken a turn, those people who hold slips read them and the people who wrote them "confess."

TIPS:

- ◆ Inform people that these will be read aloud and it is up to them to decide what they feel comfortable revealing. It may be funny or serious.
- ◆ Keep the pace brisk. It doesn't really matter if you guess right, so people should go with their first hunch rather than deliberating and slowing down the activity.
- ◆ An agreement of confidentiality is important when using this activity.

This activity was developed in the field by educators affiliated with the National School Reform Faculty.

Tools for Leaders © 2007 Marjorie Larner, Scholastic Professional

FIGURE 8-2: ACTIVITY

Tangled Hands

PURPOSE: To explore group problem-solving dynamics

1. Stand in a tight circle, very close together, with hands straight out in front of you.

2. Close your eyes and grab another person's hand with each of your hands. (Recommend that people not grab hands of people right next to them.)

3. Open your eyes and, without letting go, try to untangle until the whole group is standing in a circle. The only rule is that no one lets go of the hands they are holding.

4. Debrief: What did you learn about yourself working with a group to problem-solve? What did you notice about the dynamics of this group? How did your group respond?

This activity was developed in the field by educators affiliated with the National School Reform Faculty.

Tools for Leaders © 2007 Marjorie Larner, Scholastic Professional

FIGURE 8-3: ACTIVITY

Group Juggle

PURPOSE: To experience cooperation as a group by juggling many objects

MATERIALS: A variety of objects that vary in size and shape (such as different kinds of soft balls, small water bottles, balls of yarn, stuffed animals, large rolls of tape). Choose objects that won't hurt anyone when they make contact.

1. Ask the group to stand in a circle (6–10 people).

2. Hand one person an object and ask him or her to toss it to someone, saying that person's name as it is thrown.

3. Then that person throws the ball to another, again saying the name of that recipient.

4. Continue until everyone has had a chance to catch and throw.

5. Ask participants to remember to whom they threw the object and who threw it to them.

6. Practice the pattern once or twice.

7. Start adding one more object at a time, beginning with the same person each time with directions to repeat the same pattern so that the group is juggling several objects.

8. After a few rounds, count "1, 2, 3" and stop.

9. Debrief: What did it take for success with this task? What does this remind you of in your own professional life?

This activity was developed in the field by educators affiliated with the National School Reform Faculty.

Tools for Leaders © 2007 Marjorie Larner, Scholastic Professional

FIGURE 8-4: ACTIVITY

Diversity Rounds

PURPOSE: To become more aware of our own personal identities and the connections we have with each other; to consider the impact of diversity and personal identity.

The discussions in this protocol will have more meaning for groups that have shared experiences and developed a level of trust that allows them to go beneath the surface in what they are willing to share with one another. This activity is especially effective with large groups, such as a whole faculty.

TIME: 45–90 minutes, depending on how much time you allow for discussion

STEPS

1. The facilitator asks participants to group themselves, in turn, in four to five of the following ways (do not define the categories fully; the participants are to define for themselves the groups they form). You can choose three from the following or include some categories that relate to your group's agenda.
   - geography
   - kind of school you attended
   - role in high school
   - reform agenda identity
   - birth order
   - gender
   - ethnicity

2. As each group forms, participants discuss one or more of the following questions and prepare to report on them as a group. There will be approximately five to ten minutes for each conversation.
   - What does it mean to you to be _____?
   - How much do you define yourself this way?
   - How is this group unique/different from the other groups?
   - One thing you would like the other groups to know about us is _____.

3. Each group reports back, briefly.

4. Repeat for each category.

5. Debrief the process:
   - How did you feel about doing this exercise?
   - What did it bring up that was new for you?
   - What was difficult? What was uncomfortable? What made you feel good?
   - Would you use this activity with your students?

This protocol was developed by Nancy Mohr and Judith Scott. This version comes from *The Power of Protocols* (2003) by Joe McDonald, Nancy Mohr, Alan Dichter, and Elizabeth C. McDonald.

Tools for Leaders © 2007 Marjorie Larner, Scholastic Professional

AIM: PROVIDING RESPONSIVE FACILITATION

*Thank you for letting us do what we needed to do instead of pushing us
to follow your agenda. You really heard us say what we needed.*

— teacher reflection

The manner of facilitation impacts the tone and depth of relationships in the group through inclusion of all voices and opinions, adherence to agreements, careful listening, and, most significantly, skillful responses to the group's needs. When the group is merrily following an agenda, you might only have to help them manage time. But frequently, you will have to make judgment calls, just as you do in the classroom, between being responsive to feedback and group desires and achieving promised outcomes.

CONSIDERATIONS

When you are faced with this decision, ask yourself: What will be lost if we let go of the original plan? What do we have to gain if we follow the group's determination of what they need? How will we proceed in the best interest of the community?

When people are used to being directed, and not seen or heard, in meetings, you will get their attention and earn trust and respect if you really walk your talk about shared ownership, leadership, and the meaning of facilitation by offering options to adapt.

In the end, most people want to leave a meeting with a sense of accomplishment, so even if they have moved off topic, they are likely to eventually shift to problem solving and ideas for actions to address their challenges.

GUIDELINES FOR RESPONSIVE FACILITATION

- When people stray from the meeting's focus, offer questions and reminders to help them make conscious decisions about the direction they want to take.
- Listen carefully and check for understanding by restating what you have heard.
- Provide a suggestion or offer two options that will meet the stated needs of the group.
- Offer participants steps of an agenda, protocol, or activity so they can share responsibility for following the plan.
- Build into the agenda a designated and contained interval that ensures the opportunity to wander without letting it bleed into the whole time.
- Finally, trust that if you find you have made a decision that didn't get your group where you had hoped they would go, you will learn a lesson to use next time. Groups that have developed strong working relationships will keep striving for stronger collaboration.

Aim: Establishing a Broad Base of Support

We succeed only as we identify in life, or in war, or in anything else, a single overriding objective, and make all other considerations bend to that one objective.

— Dwight D. Eisenhower

By establishing communication, relationships, and partnerships with others beyond our group, we increase the possibilities—from gaining more financial, logistical, and problem-solving skills, to gaining a broader knowledge base and multiple perspectives.

CONSIDERATIONS

Anyone with a stake in supporting the group and achieving the goal might hold a meeting, with at least one or two representatives from the teachers' group. When it is possible, a small group of four to five people is the most efficient and productive. Whether you are meeting with administrators, colleagues, or other key people from the community, they are likely to appreciate efficient use of time for a substantive discussion.

GUIDELINES

As a facilitator, suggest an informal agenda for what you want to discuss in the meeting.

Representative from the teacher group: summarize goals, focus, purpose

- ◆ Describe how your group work is tied to the school and district goal(s).
- ◆ Ask yourself: What do you hope the group will accomplish?
- ◆ Ask yourself: What are your specific intended outcomes, particularly in terms of actions that will be taken as a result of the group's work and results for students?

Administrators respond: questions, suggestions, connections with other projects

Designated facilitator or group representative: restate what you've heard and check for common understanding

Everyone: implications for action, changes to plan, support and communication

- ◆ Resources: subs, materials, facilitator—use list from Chapter 2 (Fig. 2-1)
- ◆ Time: release days, stipends outside of contract days, commitment to support for a period of time
- ◆ Results and documentation: written report, recommendations, presentation to faculty or others, documentation of classroom change, data to be gathered

Capture in writing the agreements articulated in this meeting for future reference in tracking the process and progress. Use a graphic organizer for a visual that shows the connections and alignment. Offer the following organizer (Fig. 8-5) to each person at the meeting as a scaffold for note-taking and synthesizing the discussion. Record what you hear.

FIGURE 8-5: ORGANIZER

NOTE-TAKING

Goals, focus, purpose:

Desired outcomes:

Actions that will follow:

Connections to larger context and other projects:

New ideas for action, including resources, time, reporting:

Tools for Leaders © 2007 Marjorie Larner, Scholastic Professional

FIELD NOTES

How we listen and how we respond directly impact the quality of learning for students as well as teachers. In the following poem written by a teacher (Fig. 8-6), we see the power in a relationship resting on listening and patience. This poem actually serves dual purposes. First, it helps us remember the potential impact a teacher can have on a student's capacity to think and grow. Secondly, because aspects of the content may be disturbing to some people, it provides a real opportunity to practice understandings, skills, and structures for listening to divergent points of view. I have learned from my colleague Stevi Quate to think carefully ahead of time about laying a foundation and providing time for processing when using texts with potentially controversial content, but not to shy away from using them.

FIGURE 8-6: READING

Like Lilly Like Wilson
by Taylor Mali

I'm writing the poem that will change the
    world,
and it's Lilly Wilson at my office door.
Lilly Wilson, the recovering addict,
the worst I've ever seen.
So, like, bad the whole eighth grade
Started calling her Like Lilly Like Wilson Like.
Until I declared my classroom a Like-Free Zone,
and she could not speak for days.

But when she finally did, it was to say,
Mr. Mali, this is . . . is so hard.
Now I have to think before I . . . say anything.

Imagine that, Lilly.
It's for your own good.
Even if you don't like . . .
it.

I'm writing the poem that will change the world,
and it's Lilly Wilson at my office door.
Lilly is writing a research paper for me
about how homosexuals shouldn't be allowed
to adopt children.
I'm writing the poem that will change the world,
and it's Like Lilly Like Wilson at my office door.

She's having trouble finding sources,
Which is to say, ones that back her up.
They all argue in favor of what I thought I was
    against.

And it took four years of college,
    three years of graduate school,
    and every incidental teaching experience I have
        ever had
    to let out only,
Well, that's a real interesting problem, Lilly.
But what do you propose to do about it?
That's what I want to know.

And the eighth grade mind is a beautiful thing;
Like a newborn baby's face, you can often see it
change before your very eyes

I can't believe I'm saying this, Mr. Mali,
but I think I'd like to switch sides.

And I want to tell her to do more than just
    believe it,
but to enjoy it!
That changing your mind is one of the best
    ways
of finding out whether or not you still have one.
Or even that minds are like parachutes,
that it doesn't matter what you pack them with
    so long as they open
at the right time.
O God, Lilly I want to say
you make me feel like a teacher,
and who could ask to feel more than that?
I want to say all this but manage only
Lilly, I am like so impressed with you!

So I finally taught somebody something,
namely, how to change her mind.
And learned in the process that if I ever change
    the world
it's going to be one eighth grader at a time.

CHAPTER 9
ISSUES AND DILEMMAS: TALKING ABOUT WHAT MATTERS

To listen closely and reply well is the highest perfection we are able to attain in the art of conversation.

— François de La Rochefoucauld

How many of you share this experience that I had as a young teacher, challenged by classroom management issues?

All the other teachers were gifted veterans who wanted to help me. At lunch and in meetings, I was bombarded with beautiful ideas from my more experienced colleagues, many of which I couldn't even remember by the time I got back to my classroom, much less understand how to implement successfully. Perhaps there were one or two concrete simple suggestions, such as how to take roll, that were helpful.

My friends were also concerned and listened with great sympathy, but in the end, they also didn't help me each morning in my classroom. Looking back now, I realize what would have been most helpful to me was a coach to listen and ask questions, to help me think through what would work for me with my style and level of expertise.

AIM: USING PROTOCOLS AND SKILLS TO HELP YOU ADDRESS WHAT MATTERS

It's difficult to sit and listen to someone's problem without wanting to fix it, yet the real fix will come if you help her think in new ways, from new angles, with varying perspectives, and find a solution from within herself. There are skills you can develop and structures you can use to support this kind of helpful interaction around another person's dilemma. Two skills presented here are used in the protocols that follow at the end of this chapter. (See Fig. 9-6 and 9-8.)

In previous chapters, protocols have been suggested as a support for productive and efficient conversations. In this chapter, they support discussions that go closer to the bone, to the specifics of professional practice.

CONSIDERATIONS

While different protocols vary in significant features, they all do two things: provide a structure for conversation—a series of steps that a group follows in a fixed order—and specify the roles different people in the group will play (typically, a facilitator, a presenter, and participants). The structure of protocols is intended to encourage conversations, normally carried out within 40 minutes to a little over an hour, that are productive, inclusive, positive, and safe.

Protocols rely on a foundation of explicit agreements that every voice will be heard, every person seen, and every point of view considered. Agreement on ground rules, agendas, and structures assures inclusion of every voice in the group so it truly is a group rather than some people being actors and some being their audience.

Careful facilitation, preferably by a coach trained in collaborative processes, is the best way to help a group get started in the right direction. I have also seen that when groups are motivated to collaborate, they are able to establish conditions and effectively use these tools to meet their needs.

AIM: GETTING BUY-IN ON THE USE OF PROTOCOLS

I am ecstatic that 1) the protocols gave us common language; 2) focused planning and prep for the meeting; 3) gave everyone a voice; 4) they WORKED!
— teacher reflection

With the structure of a protocol in place to support the group's interactions, everyone shares responsibility for meaningful and relevant conversation. However, protocols are only effective when they serve the needs of the members of the group. If people do not see a purpose for following what they may see as "rules," they are unlikely to invest the protocol with the spirit of collaboration. They may hear the concept as a way to control and stifle them rather than as a support for a full conversation. It is not difficult for a person who wants to resist or even undermine a group process to do so; therefore, it is better to find willingness rather than mere acquiescence.

CONSIDERATIONS

When introducing the idea of using a structure or protocol, there are a few guidelines that make it more likely it will be received with willingness.

◆ Point out that these are tools developed by teachers to help them do what they want to do.

◆ Start by saying something to the effect of "Let's try this and see if we think it helps" or "Bear with me so you can see what it's like and then we can figure out how and where we want to use this."

◆ Explain how these structures work well with students as well as with colleagues.

◆ When you use a protocol, make sure everyone has an individual copy or that it is posted where everyone can see it easily so they can follow along, know what is coming, and not be dependent on you for each step.

Aim: Asking Questions That Prompt New Thinking

*At a preschool screening, the instructor held up a colored card and asked,
"What color is this?" The child replied, "Why? Don't you know?"*
— joke circulating among teachers

Along with listening, asking questions is a powerful tool to spark new thinking, give someone a new angle to think about their issue, or lead a person to open up to a new picture of a situation. (See Fig. 9-1.)

Learning to distinguish between different kinds of questions and determine which will be most helpful at any particular time can radically change group dynamics, especially if you are a coach or administrator supporting and guiding teachers' learning.

CONSIDERATIONS

For most of us, the natural response to hearing someone's problem is to offer a solution, and often we become invested in seeing our idea carried out. While there are certainly times when suggestions are welcome and helpful, they serve a limited purpose in the context of a collaborative learning community with long-term goals for expansion of professional capacity.

Suggestions even sneak into our questions and comments without our awareness. When you are forming your question, ask yourself:

◆ Am I looking for acceptance of my ideas rather than listening to my colleague's needs?

◆ Is the idea open-ended and general, allowing room to fill in the details, or is it specific and directive?

FIGURE 9-1: READING

TYPES OF QUESTIONS

RHETORICAL	FRAMING	CLARIFYING	PROBING
Commonly used in classrooms where students try to give the answer the teacher has in mind. Useful for evaluation; not so useful for generating thoughts and ideas.	Commonly used to focus presenter's question or dilemma to bring to colleagues. Used to clarify, narrow, get to the heart of a confusing or overwhelming issue. In the process of framing the questions, you can learn more about the issue.	Used to gather information and facts. Can usually be answered briefly or with a yes or no. Used to give a full picture in order to move to the next step fully informed of the details.	Used in protocols to help a person think from a new angle. Usually cannot be answered immediately but requires time to think. Used to get at assumptions, underlying motivations, connections, and contradictions.
Examples	**Examples**	**Examples**	**Examples**
What did I tell you was the first step toward getting approval for your plan?	What do I need to do in order to implement my plan?	Have you talked with your principal about your plan?	What is the connection between implementing your plan and the principal's perception of the situation?
Who remembers what I told you was the highest mountain in the world?	How do I work within my daily schedule to allow more choice for student work?	How many children are in the classroom?	What do you assume to be true about this student's belief about herself as a writer?
In our discussion last week, what did we decide were the events that led to the Revolutionary War?	What do I need to concentrate on if I want my students to be more responsible for doing their work?	When did you start trying to implement this new approach?	What is the connection between your dilemma and the change? What is your school going through?
	How can I support this student in his efforts to write in English (not his native language)?	What did the principal say to you?	What is your hunch about the possibilities and results of making this information public?

BACKGROUND ON PROBING QUESTIONS

A sudden, bold and unexpected question doth many times surprise a man and lay him open.
— Francis Bacon

Asking probing questions leads to a surprisingly powerful shift in the dynamics between you and the person needing help. It is a skill worth practicing. (See Fig. 9-2 and 9-3.)

FIGURE 9-2: ACTIVITY

Practicing Probing Questions

PURPOSE: To learn to develop and ask probing questions that help a presenter think about a question or dilemma

When you start out with this practice, be sure everyone understands that this is a skill that people continually work on. Practicing this skill beforehand will give people more comfort when trying out the protocol that calls for probing questions. If your group is large (more than 15), start with individuals talking in triads to generate probing questions, which then are shared with the larger group.

Give everyone a copy of Probing Questions (Fig. 9-3) to refer to as they practice.

STEPS

1. A volunteer presenter describes a dilemma or framing question. If you have time, help the volunteer clarify and frame the question.

2. Each person takes a turn asking a probing question.

3. The presenter doesn't answer the question but gives feedback as to whether it brought to light new thinking, a new angle, or a different perspective.

4. Use this opportunity to invite participants to identify and develop probing questions by encouraging discussion.

FIGURE 9-3: READING

PROBING QUESTIONS

Purpose of probing questions:

◆ To help uncover thoughts, beliefs, and opinions rather than solutions

◆ To help the presenter move beyond the original perspective or insight

◆ To help the presenter look at an issue from a new angle

Probing questions . . .

◆ do not indicate a direction or an answer.

◆ are for the benefit of the presenter, rather than the questioner.

◆ reflect a partnership between the person doing the asking and the presenter.

◆ should be interesting and challenging.

◆ should feel hard to the presenter but not so hard he or she feels pinned to the wall.

◆ might not be answerable in that moment but can be thought about over time.

When constructing probing questions, consider the following guidelines:

◆ Prepare your questions carefully before you ask them.

◆ Check to see if you have the "right" answer in mind. If so, delete the judgment from the question, or don't ask it.

◆ Refer to the presenter's original question.

◆ Check to see if you are asserting your agenda. If so, return to the presenter's agenda.

◆ Think in terms of verbs: What do you *fear*? What do you *want*? *Assume*? *Expect*?

Examples of how a probing question might start:

◆ What's your hunch about . . . ?

◆ What was your intention about . . . ?

◆ What do you assume to be true about . . . ?

◆ What would happen if . . . ?

◆ What is the connection between _____ and _____?

◆ Why is this a dilemma for you?

◆ What if the opposite were true? Then what?

Adapted from *Pocket Guide to Probing Questions*, developed by Gene Thompson-Grove, Edorah Frazer, and Faith Dunn

Protocols for Specific Aims

Each protocol provides a sequence of steps leading to specific outcomes. Read about the aims of each protocol and look over the steps to select a protocol that will structure your conversation to achieve your desired outcome.

Aim: Consulting on Dilemmas

As teachers, we face many dilemmas and difficult issues nearly every day. There are so many places these challenges can arise and so little time to think them through. You might find yourself staying up at night, circling around from one dilemma to another. Usually, it seems there is no solution or way out of the confusion and complexity. With a systematic approach, however, in a short period of time, colleagues' insights can bring new perspectives to our dilemmas. Breakthroughs are possible.

Consultancy in Triads (Fig. 9-4) is a powerful protocol that is good for a first experience because each presenter gets a personal result for something that matters to him or her, in a short period of time. Working in a small group with only two other people provides a safer and more controllable situation for revealing your vulnerability as you admit to something you don't necessarily have under control. This protocol can also be used with larger groups, with only one person presenting and more time per round for everyone to have an opportunity to speak.

Provide a graphic organizer (Fig. 9-5) to help the presenter prepare to present a dilemma and to take notes while listening to the discussion.

AIM: LEARNING FROM SUCCESS

Surprisingly and sadly, asking teachers to talk about success can be threatening and hard, for some even more so than talking about their dilemmas. People will say to me, "I have no success to talk about." To accept that would be to accept a sense of complete inadequacy and failure, and it is unlikely that could be totally true. It is more likely a habit that has served some purpose in spite of the discouragement it produces. This is actually a wonderful opportunity for you to help someone remember what he has to feel good about. If you have to, suggest looking outside of school experiences and think of any success experienced in life. Then see if you can help him make a connection to a professional success. Once you can open the door to seeing success, more memories and examples start to pop up.

Moving into triads, the small group can often encourage a hesitant colleague to admit to a success. (See Fig. 9-6.) It is so important that participants not only focus on filling in gaps, but also that they learn from what they already know—accomplishments they just thought of as "luck." But actually there are specific skills, steps, and attitudes that participants can become aware of and intentionally practice.

A triple Venn diagram could be a useful graphic organizer to identify elements of success that were different or the same in the success stories.

I always think about a participant in a summer workshop who said that starting out talking about success rather than issues and problems changed her outlook on the whole week. She remembered she had strengths to build on and her whole mood shifted from discouraged to hopeful. In recent years, researchers have begun to identify chemical changes in the brain that occur as a result of what a person thinks or experiences, with the suggestion that if you remember positive experiences, chemicals are released that bring calm and pleasure (PertEsch & Stefano, 2004).

Aim: Gathering Multiple Ideas and Perspectives

When a member of the group has a question for which she wants to hear recommendations, questions, and experiences from her colleagues, you can use the Brief Responses to Challenges protocol (Fig. 9-7) so she can hear it in an organized way to help her take it in. This simple structure forestalls the natural tendency for rapid-fire ideas coming from all directions.

When you have an agenda you are trying to follow, individual questions and concerns can derail your plans and prevent the group from meeting expectations. When a member of your group asks such a question, you can use this protocol to provide a "container" for her to get useful feedback from each person without taking over the whole meeting.

You could also use this structure for an issue concerning the whole group, for which they want to provide a chance for each person to have input. In this case, the final step of synthesizing responses could fall to a designated facilitator or other member of the group identified to listen in that way—that is, for themes, patterns, contradictions, meaning.

Aim: Project Presentation and Analysis

When you are in the midst of a project, you are probably seeing that some of what you do works well and some is not where you want it to be. Or your attention may be so deeply focused on doing the work that you don't have time to evaluate at all. The Ongoing Project Analysis protocol (Fig. 9-8) is an opportunity to describe your work, hear others' impressions of it, and consider what to continue, stop, and start. This protocol also works well as a means for faculty to be informed about what others in the building are doing.

FIGURE 9-4: PROTOCOL

Consultancy in Triads

PURPOSE: To allow individuals to think more expansively about a particular concrete dilemma

SUGGESTED TIME: 20–30 minutes for each person

Allow two to five minutes for each person to frame a dilemma and focus question to present, with these helpful guidelines:

To frame your dilemma for colleagues to help you, jot some notes and then think about what you really want to know.

- ◆ Bring something that you genuinely have not been able to figure out on your own so you will be open to new thinking.
- ◆ Focus on an issue that you can do something about rather than something that requires other people or institutions to change in order for you to address it.
- ◆ Avoid a framing question that could be answered with a yes or no.

STEPS (Read through the steps before you begin.)

1. The presenter gives an overview of the dilemma or issue, and then poses a focus question. (3 minutes)

2. The participants ask *clarifying* questions. Keep in mind that clarifying questions are primarily for the responders since these questions are aimed at helping them understand the issues and context. (2 minutes)

3. The group asks the presenter *probing* questions. Probing questions are primarily for the responders. They ask the presenter "Why?" (among other things), and are open-ended. These questions should be worded so that they help the presenter clarify and expand her thinking about the issue or question she raised for the consultancy group. The goal here is for the presenter to learn more about the question she framed or to do some analysis of the issue she presented. The presenter responds to the questions she chooses, but there is no discussion by the larger group of the presenter's responses. (5 minutes)

4. The participants talk with each other about the work and issues presented. What did we hear? What didn't we hear that we needed to know more about? What do we think about the question or issue presented? The presenter moves outside the group, silently taking notes. (5–10 minutes)

5. The presenter moves back into the group, responding to the discussion with new insights and ideas. During this time, the group remains silent. (3 minutes)

6. Open discussion. (2–5 minutes)

7. Debrief the process at the completion of all three rounds.

Developed by Gene Thompson-Grove

Tools for Leaders © 2007 Marjorie Larner, Scholastic Professional

FIGURE 9-5: ORGANIZER

CONSULTANCY ORGANIZER

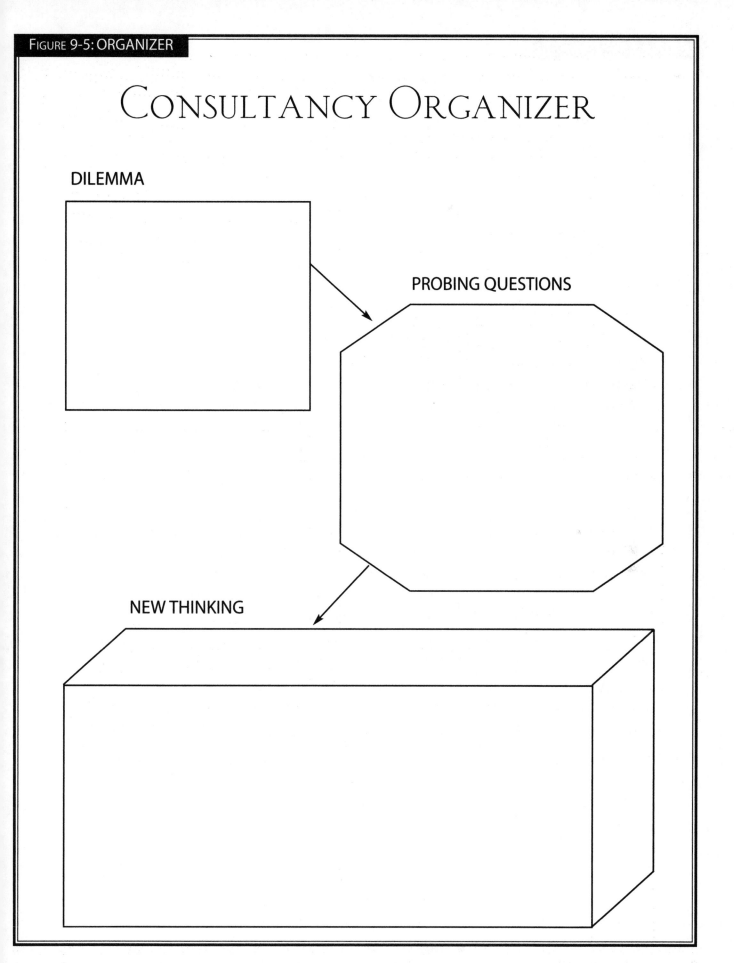

DILEMMA

PROBING QUESTIONS

NEW THINKING

FIGURE 9-6: PROTOCOL

Success Analysis Protocol

PURPOSE: To analyze what makes this self-identified practice so successful in achieving the intended outcome

STEPS (Read through the steps before you begin.)

1. Reflect on and write a short description of one "best practice" of your work within the last year. Note what it is about the practice that made it so successful. Be sure to answer the question "What made this work different from other experiences?" (2 minutes)

2. In mixed groups of three, the first person shares her or his best practice and why it was so successful. (5 minutes)

3. The rest of the group asks clarifying questions about the details of the best practice. (2 minutes)

4. The group analyzes what they heard about the presenter's success and offers additional insights about how this practice is different from other practices. Probing questions are appropriate, and the presenter may choose to include responses to these questions when she steps back in to the discussion. (5 minutes)

5. The presenter responds to the group's analysis of what made this experience so successful. (2 minutes)

6. The group takes a moment to celebrate the success of the presenter.

7. Other members of the group take turns sharing their best practices and what made them so successful, followed by clarifying questions and the group discussion analyzing how each practice differs from other practices. (Each round takes about 20 minutes for groups of three.)

8. The group analyzes common threads in all three presentations. (5–10 minutes)

9. Debrief the protocol as a whole group. Possible questions: What worked well? How might we apply what we learned to other work? How might students use this process to reflect on their work? What adaptations to this protocol might improve the process? (3–5 minutes)

Developed by Daniel Baron, www.harmonyschool.org/nsrf

Tools for Leaders © 2007 Marjorie Larner, Scholastic Professional

FIGURE 9-7: PROTOCOL

Brief Responses to Challenges

PURPOSE: To gain multiple perspectives and ideas on a pressing and discrete challenge or issue, within a short period of time

TIME: 10–20 minutes per round

STEPS (Read through the steps before you begin.)

1. The presenter describes the challenge and articulates a focus question. He or she includes context or background that is relevant and necessary for the group's understanding. (2 minutes)

2. Circle the group: Each participant offers suggestions, thoughts, perspective, further questions. (1–2 minutes each)

3. The presenter listens and takes notes.

4. The presenter (or otherwise designated person) responds: He or she synthesizes themes and patterns and lists new ideas, perspectives, and understanding. (2 minutes)

OPTIONS:

◆ The cycle is repeated until everyone in the group has had an opportunity to present.

◆ You could use this process as a structured brainstorming session.

◆ If you have more than 12 people in a group, it will take too long to go around to each person in the group. Instead, break into groups of three. Take three to five minutes for each triad to discuss their ideas and synthesize them, and then each group shares their collective ideas in the same fashion as Step 2.

◆ If you have a question that is complex, break it down into three smaller questions for three rounds of this process. (This idea comes from Academic Support and Advising at the University of Northern Colorado.)

Developed by Marjorie Larner and Ellen Miller-Brown

Tools for Leaders © 2007 Marjorie Larner, Scholastic Professional

FIGURE 9-8: PROTOCOL

Ongoing Project Analysis

PURPOSE: To provide a framework for colleagues to share significant stories of their work, with an opportunity for listeners to offer useful feedback. Depending on your situation, this protocol works well in small or large groups. You can also do several rounds so that many people get to present.

ROLES: A timekeeper/facilitator
The facilitator's role is to help the group maintain focus on the specific project and the presenter's question.

STEPS (Read through the steps before you begin.)

1. Reflect on and write a short description of one important project within the last year. Be sure to answer the question "What makes this work stand out as significant?" Note successes, concerns, challenges, accomplishment(s), and ongoing hopes for the project. Identify a focus question for colleagues to address. (2 minutes)

2. The presenter describes the project. (5 minutes)

3. The rest of the group asks clarifying questions about the details. (2 minutes)

4. The group analyzes what they have heard about the project. In round-robin style, each person offers feedback in the form of strengths of the project. Each person is allowed up to one minute, or five minutes total, for this step when working as a triad. The presenter listens and takes notes.

5. In round-robin style, the group offers insights, questions, and suggestions in regard to the presenter's question. Again, the presenter listens and takes notes. Each person is allowed up to one minute, or five minutes total, for this step when working as a triad.

6. The presenter responds to the group's analysis with initial thoughts about what to stop doing, continue doing, and start doing. (2 minutes)

7. Take a moment to celebrate the achievement of the presenter.

8. Option: other members of the group take a turn presenting their projects. (Each round takes about 20 minutes for groups of three.)

9. The group analyzes common threads in all three presentations. (5–10 minutes)

10. Debrief the protocol as a whole group. Possible questions: What worked well? How might we apply what we learned to other work? How might students use this process to reflect on their work? What adaptations to this protocol might improve the process? (3–5 minutes)

Developed by Marjorie Larner, Libby Klingsmith, and Stephanie Torrez

Tools for Leaders © 2007 Marjorie Larner, Scholastic Professional

FIELD NOTES

I have a series of e-mails that flew back and forth between a new teacher and myself as she asked for help with classroom management. I kept offering questions to help her find her own management style, while she continued to ask for techniques and strategies that she could implement the next day. She didn't have time or even space in her brain to reflect and find her own teacher presence while she was also developing everything else.

Not only was e-mail not working, but I realized that talking about it from a distance wasn't going to be enough. I needed to be in the classroom with her side by side, to help her think about what we had both seen and experienced. That in-the-trenches common ground was necessary in order for me to ask the right questions. By getting to know each other as teachers, we established a working relationship and a context for our subsequent conversations, whether on e-mail or in person. And, in a real way, she was less alone.

PART III: A CULTURE OF LEARNING

"The best thing for being sad," replied Merlin . . . "is to learn something. That is the only thing that never fails. You may grow old and trembling in your anatomies, you may lie awake at night listening to the disorder of our veins . . . you may see the world around you devastated by evil lunatics, or know your honor trampled in the sewers of baser minds. There is only one thing for it then—to learn. Learn why the world wags and what wags it. That is the only thing which the mind can never exhaust, never alienate, never be tortured by, never fear or distrust, and never dream of regretting. Learning is the thing for you."
— T. H. White, *The Once and Future King*

"The best thing for being sad . . ." I tell this to children who are struggling to find their way in school and in life, and I tell it to myself when it seems there are too many challenges to overcome. New information, fresh ideas and insights into teaching and learning, support to take risks with new instructional strategies, different perspectives on your own classrooms and students, help in working from theory to practice . . . when these conditions are met, your work together as professionals becomes an integral part of the school community, and the impact on children's learning is direct and profound.

In these chapters, you will also see more of how one process for learning is folded into another, such as reading about a particular instructional strategy prior to a classroom observation to deepen and focus perceptions, or linking observations with strategies learned from workshops to surface issues and ideas regarding implementation.

In the end, we are doing more than simply discussing a text or using a protocol in a meeting. We are sustaining a culture of learning in our schools, where it is assumed that learning is one of the joys and powers we have as human beings.

CHAPTER 10
BRINGING NEW IDEAS INTO PRACTICE: LEARNING FROM BOOKS AND WORKSHOPS

If a child is to keep alive his inborn sense of wonder, he needs the companionship
of at least one adult who can share it, rediscovering with him the joy,
excitement and mystery of the world we live in.
— Rachel Carson

I have sometimes wondered how, with all the wonderful books written and workshops offered, there always seems to be room for new books and workshops on the market. Perhaps, as in any other field of science or the arts, there is a continual search for better answers to both old and new questions.

Or is it that teachers are avid learners, just as invested in and excited about learning for themselves as they are for their students? Learning is, after all, the focus of our work lives. This aspect of my profession keeps me connected to my students' experience, sharing the struggles of not knowing, and the excitement of acquiring new skills, knowledge, and understanding.

There is a potential risk that with collaborative learning, we merely reinforce old habits and assumptions rather than move forward with new information, data, ideas, and practice.

And yet, for many of us, the demands on our time and attention make it seem nearly impossible even to begin to keep up with current literature and professional development opportunities. Or we are already overloaded with new ideas that we haven't had a chance to think about implementing.

Those of us in positions to lead and support teachers need to institute ways to ensure continuing interest, if not passion, for professional learning through relevant, valuable content and practical support to apply what is learned.

AIM: VIEWING PROFESSIONAL LEARNING AS AN IMPERATIVE FOR TEACHERS

Only people who die very young learn all they really need to know in kindergarten.
— Wendy Kaminer

Ideas of best practice in education continue to evolve and expand, as do the needs of our students. Being informed is not just a matter of choice or preference; it is imperative for teachers to explore new ideas and information and to hone their skills and expertise in order to meet current student needs.

CONSIDERATIONS

Initially, you can ensure that ongoing professional learning is part of the school culture by simply listening for questions, interests, and gaps and then offering relevant texts or new ideas. Ideally, you eventually take this further, with time set aside for focused learning experiences.

Bring text from professional literature and respected writers in the field (such as the Wiggins and McTighe excerpt in Fig. 10-1) to support your position that community learning is an imperative for success. Ask teachers to consider what this position would mean in concrete terms for them and for the school.

AIM: ESTABLISHING ROUTINES FOR READING

Read, read, read.
— William Faulkner

Professional growth depends to a great extent on professional reading, and yet it is often a challenge to make this a regular part of school life. With constant demands on teachers' time and attention, is reading really so important? If it is, then how do busy teachers fit it into their days?

CONSIDERATIONS

I have heard teachers say, "I never read." Others say they have stacks of books by their bed that they can't get to, and still others somehow seem to keep up with all the latest, greatest books. In this continuum, where would you put yourself? If you read, what do you read, and for what purpose?

FIGURE 10-1: ACTIVITY

Reading With Guiding Questions

Allow time for people to read this short excerpt with these questions in mind for discussion after reading:

◆ What does this mean for you?

◆ What would it mean for our team, our school?

◆ Include concrete examples in the discussion.

Examining the Teaching Life

We need to assess teaching practices and professional development activities in light of sound principles about how learning works.

A school is in business to promote learning. It should therefore model for all institutions what it means to be a learning organization. A school is not merely a place that expects students to learn; it must encourage and support everyone's learning.

For a school to be a model learning organization, all faculty members should be professional learners: They should engage in deep, broad study of the learning they are charged to cause. What works? What doesn't? Where is student learning most successful, and why? How can we learn from that success? Where are students struggling to learn, and why? What can we do about it? Effectively tackling these questions is what the "professional" in "professional practice" means. (Wiggins & McTighe, 2006)

Tools for Leaders © 2007 Marjorie Larner, Scholastic Professional

Over the years, I have compiled responses from both teachers and students to this question. I bring this compilation to students as a prompt for their thinking about why they would choose to read. I think this is a pretty persuasive argument for reading as a crucial component of learning for people of all ages.

◆ Reading is one of the most efficient and effective methods we have for accessing new information.

◆ Reading allows time for deliberation and reflection on new ideas. You can mark a place to come back to reread and reconsider.

◆ You can have a conversation with the writer, argue, agree, clarify your own thoughts.

◆ Everyone can read the same information for a common base in a discussion.

◆ The text can back up your position because it doesn't change; it will be there when you want to go back and make reference to it.

◆ There are so many wonderful sources from which to choose what is just right for you.

GUIDELINES FOR SELECTING TEXT

One of the great perks when you are no longer a student in school is that you can choose when and what you want to read. So we need to work within that reality, and honor the autonomy of adult professionals to choose what is worthwhile for them to read. However, I would never leave out the possibility of new discoveries when you listen to recommendations or respond to pressure and try texts you would not have otherwise considered. Guidelines for selecting text for your group sessions follow.

◆ When you choose a text that addresses your group's questions and situation, they are more likely to stay with it. A group of teachers who wanted to look at subtle ways their behaviors and language affected their students' belief in themselves as learners read *Choice Words* by Peter H. Johnston. This is a short book packed with classroom-based insights and examples, organized in such a way that it was easy to read small sections at a time through the course of a semester.

◆ Think outside the usual choices for texts that may come from other fields. Books written for the business world such as *The Tipping Point* by Malcolm Gladwell and *From Good to Great* by Jim Collins offer insights and frameworks to help you view how systems change when you are going through whole-school reform.

◆ Look for powerful stories, biographies, and memoirs. You can find many short stories in young adult fiction, from authors such as Gary Soto or Sandra Cisneros, to prime the pump for observing students or looking at student work. Ask your school librarian for suggestions.

◆ Tie reading selection to learning outcomes such as discovering specific strategies or concrete ideas, sparking and inspiring new ways of thinking, and deepening content knowledge.

◆ Ask for suggestions from the group. If you want to formalize this request, ask each person to bring in one recommendation that is relevant to your work. You will end up with a useful bibliography of recommended readings for teachers. Your school librarian may have

---

To Teachers

I remember a friend pushing me to read *The Life of Pi* by Yann Martel, though I had twice rejected it, after skimming a couple of pages, as of no interest to me. But my friend Sam, with all the power of her enthusiasm and certainty, said, "You have to get through the first hundred pages and I promise you will love it." I trusted her opinion and struggled through the first hundred pages; then, just as she promised, I became enthralled with the writing, the characters, and the story.

What assigned or recommended reading has had unexpected value for you? As a child? As an adult? Who or what helped you find value in a challenging book?

funds to purchase or locate these materials for your professional library.

◆ Collect quotes, poems, and short paragraphs that take only a minute to read and still provide great material for discussion. Look for them among your own favorite writers, biographies, or poetry anthologies. You can also find poems with particular themes through relatively quick Internet searches. For instance, in a couple minutes, by typing in "quotes on reading," I was able to select three quotes to kick off a provocative conversation about reading comprehension with high school language arts teachers. I asked them to choose a quote and share what it meant to them, which led to a discussion about how they taught and used reading in their L.A. classrooms. Not only did the quotes, some of which follow, provide a focal point for our discussion, but teachers used them with their students for a similar discussion in their classrooms.

The book to read is not the one which thinks for you, but the one which makes you think. — James McCosh

I have often reflected upon the new vistas that reading opened to me. I knew right there in prison that reading had changed forever the course of my life. As I see it today, the ability to read awoke in me some long dormant craving to be mentally alive. — Malcolm X

To read without reflecting is like eating without digesting. — Edmund Burke

◆ Identify a purpose while reading, such as sharing a quote or excerpt that is especially significant, or generating a list of strategies, concepts, or key ideas to be shared with the group after reading.

GUIDELINES: LOGISTICAL SOLUTIONS TO CARVE OUT TIME FOR READING

◆ Set aside time in meetings for people to read. (Allow 5 to 10 minutes for two pages.)

◆ Read the text, if it is no more than two and a half pages, a paragraph at a time round-robin style, to have a shared experience of hearing the words. This also brings every voice into the room.

◆ Choose short, targeted texts rather than long, broad texts.

◆ Use a jigsaw approach when there is a lot of territory to cover, with everyone teaching each other what they've learned, to cut down on the amount of time spent reading.

◆ Use structures and protocols that provide guidelines for meaningful discussion of the text within your time frame and focus.

◆ Start a meeting with a discussion of the reading if you notice that your group tends to stay in issue discussions, never getting around to discussing the reading.

◆ Tie the reading to an activity that follows immediately, such as a classroom observation, to give the reading and discussion more purpose and practicality.

AIM: APPLICATION FROM WORKSHOPS

To be effective, professional development provides teachers with a way to directly apply what they learn to their teaching. Research shows that professional development leads to better instruction and improved student learning when it connects to the curriculum materials that teachers use, the district and state academic standards that guide their work, and the assessment and accountability measures that evaluate their success.

— Wiggins and McTighe

A few years ago I attended a workshop with a group of teachers I was coaching. The presenter was dynamic and every idea resonated with what we were trying to do in their classrooms. We were inspired and excited. When the workshop ended, we walked out together, talking fast about what we could do back at school. It was Friday afternoon. By Monday, there was a crisis with new students, planning for back-to-school night the next day, and an outdoor-education trip coming up the following week. We never found time to talk about implementation of all those great ideas and they were, eventually, lost to us as well as to our colleagues who were waiting to hear what we had learned.

I vowed I would not let this happen again. Since then, I have worked with principals to find time on in-service days, during common planning time, and in faculty meetings to ensure that learning in workshops will be transferred to the classrooms.

By committing time and support for teachers to share what they've learned and to collaboratively problem-solve and generate ideas for implementation, you not only make it possible for real change to occur, you also convey a message of authentic commitment to implementation of the workshop material. (See Fig. 10-2.)

FIGURE 10-2: PROTOCOL

Debrief a Workshop

PURPOSE: When only a few teachers attend a workshop, ensure a chance for them to talk and articulate what was of value and use.

TIME: With a clear focus, 30 minutes can be an adequate amount of time.

STEPS

1. Establish time frames for the discussion.

2. Each person shares his or her significant memories of the workshop.

3. Each person shares his or her ideas for classroom application.

4. The group brainstorms potential benefit to the school, particularly meeting school goals or district mandates.

Tools for Leaders © 2007 Marjorie Larner, Scholastic Professional

CONSIDERATIONS

Workshops, trainings, conferences, and institutes have become a regular part of many teachers' school years. Increasingly, opportunities for these kinds of experiences are tied to district or state goals and programs. Even when participants are excited about the new ideas and eagerly look forward to the potential improvement in their practice, the reality back at school can be that you are swept up in the day-to-day work with no time or space to figure out how these new ideas connect to what is already in place. This takes a toll on teacher time and sense of efficacy.

SCHOOLWIDE DISSEMINATION OF LEARNING FROM A WORKSHOP

The following agenda (Fig. 10-3) is an example of a plan for teachers who have attended a workshop to "teach" their colleagues what they have learned. These teachers who will present meet beforehand to create the agenda. With a structure such as in this example, the plan can be developed within 30–60 minutes. You will need to decide:

◆ **Content:** What did you learn that will be helpful to your colleagues?

◆ **Process:** What did you experience in the workshop that you would like to replicate for colleagues?

◆ **Responsibilities:** In the following agenda, each workshop attendee takes responsibility for teaching one aspect of what he or she has learned, including implementation ideas and experiences. One of the benefits is that teachers hear from a colleague who shares excitement and practical advice. If possible, let each presenter choose the element to teach. Teachers working in pairs can support each other in taking this risk of

FIGURE 10-3

EXAMPLE AGENDA

AGENDA

Date: November 2005

Focus: Implementation of instructional strategies learned in workshop

TIME	AGENDA	COMMENT/NOTES
8:30–8:50 A.M.	Greetings Overview of the day & schedule distributed Teachers are grouped	Refreshments
8:50–9:00 A.M.	Move to first center	Administrators and coaches available to answer questions
9:00–9:50 A.M.	Center 1	
9:50–10:00 A.M.	Move to second center	
10:00–10:50 A.M.	Center 2	
10:50–11:00 A.M.	Move to third center	
11:00–11:50 A.M.	Center 3	
11:50 A.M.– 1:00 P.M.	Return for whole group debrief and lunch	Time to talk on their own and come together at the end. Prompt: Share ideas for application. Chart?
1:00–2:45 P.M.	Team Meetings or work in classrooms	Ask everyone to include at least one step for application from morning learning
2:45–3:15 P.M.	Return to whole group: Written reflections on the day. Volunteers share.	What did you learn that you will apply? What worked well for you today? What would you do differently next time?

teaching their own colleagues.

◆ **Organization:** In this example, teachers rotate through three "centers," with a chance to experience each one through the course of a morning. If you have more than three centers or a large faculty, or if you want to allow a longer chunk of time to go more deeply into particular topics, teachers could sign up for the topics of interest to them rather than going to each one.

SHARING IDEAS FOR IMPLEMENTATION WITH TEAMS OR SMALL GROUPS

This format (Fig. 10-4) works well for smaller groups of teachers, perhaps grade-level teams, to build a collective body of knowledge and understanding about implementation when not everyone has attended a workshop or training. With a new math program implementation on the horizon, for example, colleagues could help one another make the shift. You could work with your principal to monitor progress and provide help where more support might be needed. Others who did not attend particular workshops might have attended related workshops in the past that they can bring to the conversation.

The main purpose is to fit the sharing into time that is available without having to rearrange schedules. Depending on the depth and amount of information to convey and the interest among teachers, this could involve one short meeting over lunch or after school, or it could be carried over from one common planning meeting or faculty meeting to another that continues to look at implementation.

FIGURE 10-4: PROTOCOL

Sharing Ideas for Implementation

PURPOSE: To extend successful practice to everyone in the building

STEPS (Read through steps before you begin.)

1. The presenter describes what he or she learned, including changes in practice: plans, actions, anticipated or experienced challenges, materials needed or created. If student work as a result of this innovation is available, it is shared with the group at this time.

2. Ideas are recorded to create a notebook of implementation strategies available to all faculty.

3. The group asks questions. Members of the group make connections to their own practice and share ideas for how they could use this new learning.

4. Recommendations for support, further learning, reading, training, and discussion are generated.

5. The group may continue to allow others to present, if time allows, in rounds of 20–30 minutes.

FOLLOW-UP:

◆ Consider doing School Walks (see Chapter 11, Fig. 11-11), which focus on recording evidence of implementation. This hones everyone's observational skills and ability to identify evidence. What does a classroom implementing this math program look like? What does schoolwide implementation look like?

◆ Undertake classroom observations to share and explore implementation (see Chapter 11).

Tools for Leaders © 2007 Marjorie Larner, Scholastic Professional

IN-SCHOOL PROFESSIONAL DEVELOPMENT DAYS

I hope when I die it will be at an in-service. It will be an easy transition from life to death.
— joke circulating on the Internet for years

Do you hate it when the district takes over your in-service days, or do you worry over what to do with them when it is up to you to plan and facilitate? Many principals and coaches have been thinking outside the usual professional development box to create meaningful collaborative work experiences that are practical as well as reenergizing for individuals and for the school community.

With careful planning, these days offer tremendous opportunity for teachers to come together and share in learning that can be tailored to their school and made directly applicable to the classroom. (See Fig. 10-5 and 10-6 for a template and an example.)

FIGURE 10-5: ORGANIZER

AGENDA TEMPLATE
Professional Development Day With Choice of Focus

TIME	AGENDA	COMMENT/NOTES
9:00 – 9:30 A.M.	Greetings, refreshments, and selection of options for the day. Sign up for one or more options. Common text:	
9:30 – 9:45 A.M.	**BREAK**	
9:45 – 11:00 A.M.	**OPTION 1** Reading and discussion: Activity: Reflection: Please bring:	
11:00 A.M. – 12:15 P.M.	**OPTION 2** Reading and discussion: Activity: Reflection: Please bring:	
12:15 – 1:00 P.M.	**LUNCH**	
1:00 – 2:15 P.M.	**OPTION 3** Reading and discussion: Activity: Reflection: Please bring:	
2:15 – 3:15 P.M.	Debrief and plan.	

Additional Instructions

FIGURE 10-6

EXAMPLE AGENDA

AGENDA: PROFESSIONAL DEVELOPMENT DAY

TIME	AGENDA	COMMENT/NOTES
9:00–9:30 A.M.	Meet in library for refreshments, greetings, and selection of options for the day. Sign up for one or more options. Common text: *Exploring Foundations*, Ritchhart	• Options are posted on wall • Markers • Be available to help people choose • Pick up snacks
9:30–9:45 A.M.	**BREAK**	

9:45–11:00 A.M.	**Writing and Beliefs**
	How do our beliefs inform our teaching? We will revisit beliefs identified in the fall and consider how these inform our teaching practice and what we can do to increase congruence of beliefs and practice.
	1. Reading and discussion of text
	2. Discussion of beliefs
	3. Chart—beliefs and actions (current and desired)
	4. How do we increase congruence of our beliefs and our practice?
	5. We believe _____ and so we _____.
	Please bring:
	  • Belief statement from the fall
	  • Pen and paper
		Bring copies of document from Beliefs discussion—offer oral summary

11:00 A.M.–12:15 P.M.	**Teachers as Writers**
	Constructing our own body of knowledge about learning to write: We will learn about teaching writing through metacognition of our own experience.
	1. Reading and discussion
	2. 10–15 minutes writing from a prompt
	3. Consider what we can learn from our own writing process. What helped us write? What got in the way?
	4. If there is time and interest and if anyone would like to bring a student writing sample to the group, we can use a process to learn through looking at student work.
	5. Identify implications and recommendations for what we as teachers do and provide for children learning to write.
	Please bring:
	  • Pen and paper
	  • Student writing sample (optional)
		• 2 options for prompts
		• Use a prompt we give students

FIGURE 10-6, PAGE 2

TIME	AGENDA	COMMENT/NOTES
12:15–1:00 P.M.	**LUNCH**	
1:00–2:15 P.M.	**Response to Classroom Crisis** Develop an action plan for students presenting severe challenges in the classroom. 1. Reading and discussion 2. Consultancy protocol to address these focus questions: How do we as a school and community and as individual adults respond both proactively and reactively to challenges we are facing with particular children so that they are safe and all the children in the school continue to feel safe? How do we minimize disruption of learning in the school? How do we maximize benefit for everyone? 3. Generate ideas to go into the action plan. Please bring: pen and paper.	*Reminder of norms—especially confidentiality*
2:15–3:15 P.M.	The Leadership Team reconvenes to debrief—for everyone who was part of this group last year and anyone who would like to join this year. We will look at plans and goals for individual and community development for the upcoming year.	*Bring notes from last year's meetings to reference*

CONSIDERATIONS

With your plan, think about how to promote focus and efficiency while allowing for thoughtful exploration, interaction, and inclusion. It is possible to plan an in-service day in which a morning is sufficient for the content, so teachers can spend the afternoon in their classrooms or meeting in teams to begin the application step of learning. I have seen teachers go back after one of these mornings and totally rearrange their classroom in order to implement a new way of teaching the next school day.

GUIDELINES

◆ Allow for choice when possible, even when the content is about a program or approach that everyone will be expected to learn and implement. You can offer choices of which particular aspects to work on that day.

◆ Find time slots that align with current schedules: in-service days, faculty meetings, common planning times, team meetings.

◆ Think in increments of time that allow for changes in activity and focus, over the course of a meeting or throughout the day. There is more energy when everyone keeps moving and when they know they are getting a concise and focused set of skills, concepts, and activities that their colleagues have found useful. Consider using only part of an in-service day or faculty meeting for new learning, leaving substantial time for practical tasks, or bookend classroom or planning time with professional learning activities.

◆ Consider ways to create smaller groups with more opportunity for differentiation according to individual needs. Offer choices that allow teachers to spend their time in groups that they self-select by interest or affinity, grade level or mixed grade, diverse or random groups.

MAKING TIME FOR PROFESSIONAL LEARNING IN FACULTY MEETINGS

Recognizing the tension between all the different demands on time at faculty meetings, even if business or other topics must be covered, there are still ways to regularly include time for professional learning.

1. Begin meetings with 10 to 15 minutes for people to share their experiences implementing new ideas or programs. Use a connections process with constructivist listening (see Chapter 7) if you don't want to take time for discussion or venting. Note challenges to address at another time.

2. Begin meetings with ten minutes of brief celebrations of success, asking especially for anything involving the new program or ideas.

3. One teacher or team then shares a success in detail, leading everyone through the classroom activity with time for discussion.

4. Share a reading or idea from a workshop, with a text-based discussion in small groups.

PRESENTATIONS

Make sure you have finished speaking before your audience has finished listening.
— Dorothy Sarnoff

As a coach, principal, or teacher leader, you are likely to stay current with the latest research and professional literature as well as have opportunities to attend workshops, conferences, and meetings. It is expected that you will bring the learning back to the teachers in your school, who may receive the information with varying degrees of openness, interest, resistance, or opposition.

CONSIDERATIONS

The chances of more successful sharing experiences are higher if you give participants time to be active in the learning—to think, talk, ask questions, and brainstorm connections and implications for practice—and ease into gradual rather than immediate implementation.

GUIDELINES

◆ Present the new ideas in practice, as a demonstration lesson for teachers to observe and discuss.

◆ Offer to bring new ideas to teachers' classrooms and try them out together.

◆ Share informally with enthusiasm and excitement but not as a hard sell.

◆ Present in short segments at faculty meetings or in-service days.

◆ Meet with teams to tell them about what you have learned and how you can help them bring it into their classrooms.

◆ Present new materials when there is time for teachers to look them over and discuss them.

AIM: IMPLEMENTING PROFESSIONAL LEARNING

Committing to implementation is obviously an essential aspect of professional learning. A tight focus and a powerful reading or idea with collaborative processes for dialogue can bring members of a group together in a short period of time to support one another in successful implementation of new learning.

CONSIDERATIONS

With carefully structured activities, you can facilitate a sequence where teachers read and discuss a new instructional strategy from a workshop, text, etc., sketch out a plan, and get feedback on the plan, all within 60 to 90 minutes. (See Fig. 10-7 and 10-8.) This would be a good structure for a team to use during a common planning time, if there is a particular strategy or lesson each member would like to add to his or her repertoire. If you combine this sequence with classroom observations of a lesson (see Chapter 11), you would have a version of a lesson study such as, "a [collaborative] professional development process that Japanese teachers engage in to systematically examine their practice, with the goal of becoming more effective" (Lesson Study Research Group, n.d.).

Figure 10-7: Protocol

Professional Learning Cycle Activity

Purpose: Work together to implement learning from common readings

Time: 60–90 minutes

Steps

1. Identify a source of new ideas for the classroom.
    - Strategy or approach from workshop that can be described on paper
    - Short text that can be read in under ten minutes at your meeting. The best texts for this purpose include a short rationale or philosophical statement followed by explicit activity-implementation ideas. Examples include:

        Action Strategies by Jeffrey Wilhelm

        Subjects Matter by Steve Zemelman and Harvey Daniels

        The Comprehension Toolkit: Language and Lessons for Active Literacy by Stephanie Harvey and
        Anne Goudvis

        The Reading Zone by Nancie Atwell

        Choice Words: How Our Language Affects Children's Thinking by Peter Johnston

2. Allow 5–10 minutes to read. Give directions that you will be using the Text Rendering protocol (Chapter 7, Fig. 7-3) to start the discussion, so they will want to identify a sentence, a phrase, and a word that stands out to them. (5–7 minutes)

3. Use the Text Rendering protocol, followed by discussion. (20 minutes)

4. Participants sketch a plan with these directions: take some time to work by yourself or with a partner or team to think about how you would integrate this strategy into your classroom in the near future. Stress that there is intentionally time only for a sketch so you can still get feedback in the next step. (20–30 minutes)

5. Ask volunteers to present plans. Depending on how many people are in your group, you can break into smaller groups of no fewer than four and use the Tuning Protocol (Fig. 10-8) to get feedback on your plan.
    Option: Some groups like to stay together, and if more than one person wants to present, use your judgment to modify and shorten the protocol for each person.

6. Debrief and plan for follow-up to hear about implementation experiences and insights.

Developed by Colorado Critical Friends Group, www.coloradocfg.org

Tools for Leaders © 2007 Marjorie Larner, Scholastic Professional

FIGURE 10-8: PROTOCOL

Tuning Protocol

PURPOSE: To provide feedback so a plan can be revised

TIME: 25–30 minutes

FACILITATOR: Helps group allow everyone to speak and stay within time frame

STEPS (Read the steps before you begin.)

1. Examine or listen to a description of the plan. (5 minutes)

2. Ask clarifying questions in round-robin style. (2 minutes)

   The purpose of these questions is to ensure the responders understand the question/concern. Bear in mind the following:

   ◆ Clarifying questions refer to facts.

   ◆ Avoid questions that hint of judgment.

3. Ask probing questions. (3 minutes)

   The purpose of these questions is for the presenter to think more deeply about the work.

4. The group offers feedback. (10 minutes)

   ◆ Solicit warm or positive comments: What are the strengths of this work?

   ◆ Ask for cool, not cruel, comments: What questions does the work provoke? Are there gaps?

5. The presenter shares new thoughts about the project. (3 minutes)

6. Recommendations (5 minutes)

7. Debrief.

Developed by Joseph MacDonald and David Allen

Tools for Leaders © 2007 Marjorie Larner, Scholastic Professional

FIELD NOTES

After a demonstration lesson under less than ideal circumstances did not go exactly according to plan, I said to the teachers in the debrief, "I learned so much from that!" Before I could start listing all I had learned, a teacher interrupted me, "You learned? You're supposed to know it all!"

Everyone waited to see what my reaction would be. I looked in vain for an exit, either physical or metaphorical. Luckily, the teacher in me rose to the surface and I went for the opportunity of a learning experience. "What were you expecting to see," I asked the group, "if all had been perfect? What was missing from this picture?" They talked about what they had read in the book we were using in a study group. Then we speculated as to why things went the way they did (from classroom conditions, time, and student dispositions, to my actions) and what would have had to change to make it fit the more perfect picture.

Although I preferred the times when my demo lessons were flawless, the students brilliant and focused and the teachers impressed and inspired, this experience where we were all knocked off balance actually provoked more problem solving, analyzing, and perceived need for further reading.

I learned to be explicit about my role as a catalyst for learning rather than the know-it-all of teaching. I wanted to model being a learner, sharing new ideas from reading and workshops and experiences, as much as I modeled being a teacher, sharing strategies, skills, and programs.

I think that this understanding has become widespread as we have moved from a model of staff development, in which something is done and brought to passive teachers, to a current model of coaching and facilitation of teachers' active learning.

CHAPTER 11
CLASSROOM
OBSERVATIONS

The desk is a dangerous place from which to watch the world.
— John Le Carré

For many years now, I've been hearing statements about the need to make teaching public, to open classroom doors, to end the isolation. I am seeing this happening with increasing frequency in all kinds of schools. Once teachers get over what for some is initial nervousness, the reward of sharing real experience and feeling like they're part of a team rather than all on their own makes this one of their most requested formats for professional development.

When you see each other's classrooms, perhaps the very kids you've talked with one another about, you might be surprised and validated by the feedback and perceptions. Your eyes may be opened to totally new ways of seeing your students. You'll get to know one another and your situations so much better when you see them for yourselves rather than through secondhand accounts.

When you use a formalized process to walk through your own buildings with a particular question or focus, you can get a sense of the big picture as well as the details you might otherwise miss as you rush through your days. You can see where there is consistency from classroom to classroom, in the hallways, in the cafeteria, gym, and schoolyard, creating a coherent culture to support the people in the building.

Through a discovery and data-gathering process using observations, data from tests and other assessments, school statistics, anecdotal records, and student work (see Chapter 12), you and the teachers with whom you work construct your own collective body of knowledge directly related to application in your school context.

Aim: Introducing the Benefit of Observations

The great aim of education is not knowledge but action.
— Herbert Spencer

The prospect of opening the classroom to other eyes often causes concern or discomfort for teachers who are used to working in private, behind closed doors.

Starting with a short article from another field, you can establish a potential purpose that is greater than the potential risk, without making anyone defensive about his or her own practice. (See Fig. 11-1.)

When you have finished reading and discussing the article, prompt a discussion with this statement: A teacher's job is as serious as a surgeon's, perhaps as much a matter of life and death, though the results of a teacher's actions may take years to appear.

Aim: Creating Conditions for Learning from Observations

We don't see things as they are, we see things as we are.
— Anaïs Nin

The rewards of peer review and feedback come from concrete, relevant learning inherent in such an experience. The risk comes in not being able to control what observers see and what they will reflect back about their observations. Before observing, there are safeguards and conditions you can put in place to minimize risk and maximize reward through discussions and agreements.

For teachers who are not accustomed to opening the doors of their classrooms, the prospect of being observed, as well as observing, can raise anxiety levels. It is helpful to acknowledge that risk and varying levels of comfort are involved and to offer a framework to talk about the level of that risk for each individual in order to manage it for maximal learning. The two activities that follow (Fig. 11-2 and 11-3) provide a structure for individuals to become aware of how they feel about an experience and for the group to share their hopes and concerns in a way that can inform planning and actions the group will take.

FIGURE 11-1: READING

Cooperating to Cut Bypass Deaths

CHICAGO, March 19 (AP)—Applying industrial management techniques to medicine, a group of surgeons saw the death rate among their heart-bypass patients fall by one-fourth after observing one another in the operating room and sharing their know-how.

"We didn't invent any treatment," said Dr. Gerald T. O'Connor of Dartmouth Medical School in Lebanon, N.H., an epidemiologist. "We got better at doing the things we already do." Dr. O'Connor's report on the project appears on Wednesday's issue of The Journal of the American Medical Association.

All 23 participating heart surgeons in Maine, New Hampshire and Vermont took part in the project. It also included nonsurgical heart doctors, anesthesiologists, nurses and aides at all five of the medical centers that provide bypass operations in the three states.

The doctors spent nine months cooperating intensely, using methods made famous by W. Edwards Deming, an industrial consultant whose theories emphasizing teamwork and communication over competition, are widely applied in industry in Japan and the United States.

Dr. O'Connor noted that doctors usually function like individual craftsmen, without sharing information about how they practice. In the study, however, teams from each hospital visited all the other medical centers, observed operations and wrote reports comparing what they saw with methods at their home centers. All results were shared, and institutions and doctors adopted changes in the scores of steps in cardiac surgery that they thought were beneficial.

For example, one institution might have changed the way breathing tubes were removed after surgery, another the position of the heart-lung machine in the operating room and a third the type of antibiotic used.

The study compared overall death rates in the three years before the cooperation with the two years and three months afterward, during which the hospitals continued to communicate but stopped the structured visits and meetings.

The death rate in the first three years was 4.4 percent, while in the second period, it was 3.6 percent.

The 6,500 patients in the second period were generally older and sicker and needed bypasses more urgently than patients in the first three years, and the expected death rate was 4.7 percent for the final period.

"There were 234 observed deaths, while 308 were expected," the researchers said. "This 24 percent reduction in mortality rates represents 74 deaths."

Dr. O'Connor said he believed the methods used in New England could be applied in other parts of the country and in other fields, such as orthopedics, brain surgery or cancer treatment. But outside experts who praised the work said it will be hard to get doctors to change.

"Will human beings actually do this?" asked Dr. Sankey V. Williams, a researcher into heart bypass death rates and a professor of medicine at the Hospital of the University of Pennsylvania. "Not until they're forced." *(Associated Press, 1996).*

FIGURE 11-2: ACTIVITY

Zones of Comfort, Risk, and Danger

Draw concentric circles on big paper posted on a wall or use masking tape to create concentric circles on the floor.

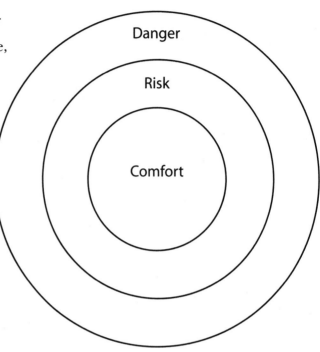

- ◆ Explain that the inner circle is the Zone of Comfort, where you do what is comfortable, which doesn't require any stretching or learning.

- ◆ Explain that the next ring represents the Zone of Risk, where you aren't always sure you know what to do as you are stretching into new territory. This is where the brain's synapses are firing, where a lot of activity and growth occurs.

- ◆ Explain that the outer ring represents the Zone of Danger, where you are just trying to survive and cannot pay attention to anything else, much less something new.

- ◆ Offer a series of scenarios, one at a time, and ask participants: Where would you place yourself in this situation?

- ◆ Participants either move to that spot if the circles are on the floor, or place a sticky dot on the circles drawn on paper. Ask volunteers to share why they would place themselves in a particular spot. Ask them what it would take to move from one ring of the circle to another.

Note: It is helpful to use a metaphor involving a physical activity to really grasp the impact on the potential for learning. You might start off with scenarios not related to observing, such as singing alone in the shower, singing with friends, and singing alone in front of a thousand people, before moving on to scenarios more directly related to your work together. Once you get to the point of talking about the particular work you will be doing, such as observing and being observed, you can ask for specific ideas from each person in regard to being in a zone for learning.

The concept of zones of comfort, risk, and danger provides a framework for the group to refer to in your ongoing work together, so allow time for each person to get a solid understanding of what it means.

Provided to the National School Reform Faculty by Marylyn Wentworth

FIGURE 11-3: ACTIVITY

Continuum Activity

STEPS

1. Explain that you will be asking everyone to respond to hypothetical situations or personal preferences by placing themselves on a continuum along an arc that you provide on individual pieces of paper, chart paper on the wall, or with an imaginary line on the floor where they actually stand.

2. Ask participants: Where would you put yourself along the continuum in terms of comfort with . . .? Allow people to talk informally to each other and ask volunteers to explain their positions.

3. Continue with more scenarios, such as specific kinds of observations and where they would place themselves on the continuum (choose two or three from this list or examples that apply):
   ◆ General observation of teacher
   ◆ Observation of teacher with specific questions regarding her effectiveness
   ◆ Demonstration lesson to gain ideas from her about "best practices"
   ◆ Observation of teacher to gain ideas about how to use a specific strategy
   ◆ Observation of student-teacher interactions to offer her feedback and ideas
   ◆ Observation of students with essential guiding questions for everyone's learning

4. Ask volunteers at different places along the continuum to explain why they chose their particular spot and what would lead them to feel safer.

5. As a group, make adjustments to your observation plan based on this discussion, to accommodate the level of risk that will work for your group. Change some aspect of the observation in question, such as the focus, who is observing, or when you observe.

Developed by Marylyn Wentworth

Tools for Leaders © 2007 Marjorie Larner, Scholastic Professional

AGREEMENTS FOR OBSERVING

Observing, note taking, and debriefing, with agreements in place that ensure safely communicated useful information, are essential components for teachers engaged in any collaborative endeavor for learning.

Before the observation, there are certain questions that usually arise having to do with the degree of interaction with students, time allowed, and placement of observers around the room and their interaction with one another. These rules are best discussed in the context of meeting the purpose of the observation and ensuring the comfort level of the observed teacher and students. Offer a sample list of agreements for the group to consider and revise to fit your needs.

To Teachers

You might not realize the effect of the presence of extra adults on children in the classroom. Even when children are working and talking in groups, when adults also begin talking, the noise level inevitably becomes unmanageable. Unless the teacher has a specific request that requires you to talk with the students, you want to have as little impact on the classroom as possible so you can see things as they would usually occur.

Sample Agreements for Observing

◆ Be a fly on the wall: this is not a time for you to teach but to sit back and enjoy watching without responsibility.

◆ Lean in close so you can hear and see.

◆ Feel free to step out of the room when you need to, such as when you want to have a conversation.

◆ Focus on one: choose one student, one instructional strategy, one question at a time for your observation and note taking.

AIM: PROVIDE A FOCUS

Questions propel us forward and take us deeper.
— Stephanie Harvey and Anne Goudvis

Learning is meaningful when it touches on our curiosity or wonder, when it matches what we are looking to know more about. With an opportunity to think about and articulate our questions, we prepare ourselves for getting the most learning out of observing in classrooms. Genuine self-generated questions are more likely to appeal to a group's interests and needs, leading them to take the risk of participating. They will also be more likely to take responsibility, invest their best effort, and figure out subsequent application.

CONSIDERATIONS

There are endless directions these questions can take, including but not limited to the following:

- Specific aspects of instruction or classroom management
- Essential questions about teaching and learning
- Focus on students to open up a picture of what they are doing in class
- Instructional moves, approaches, and strategies

SAMPLE QUESTIONS TO FOCUS AN OBSERVATION

- What are students being asked to do and how are they being asked to do it?
- What instructional strategies do we notice that provide entry points for the range of students in the classroom, and how are students responding to these? Possible strategies might include: pre-teaching, differentiating, questioning, visual as well as oral communications, other sheltering techniques.
- What skills, background knowledge, habits, academic language, and content knowledge do students need in order to do what they are being asked?
- What are students doing? Possible observable behaviors might include responding to teacher questions, talking one-on-one with the teacher or another student, copying from a model provided by the teacher or someone else, listening, taking notes, and reading.

BEFORE THE OBSERVATION

1. The group brainstorms essential questions about teaching and learning.
2. Each person chooses one question as a focus for the observation.
3. Plan to spend 40–60 minutes in the classroom observing. Remind observers to script

TROUBLESHOOTING: OBSERVING CONSTRUCTIVELY, NOT DESTRUCTIVELY

If you go in just observing a teacher's general instruction, you may come too close to what happens in a teacher evaluation, or your observations may wander, leading to vague feedback. Make the most productive use of the time you have with an explicit, clear focus and purpose. Be very clear this observation is for learning, and the only feedback that will come close to evaluating an individual teacher's efficacy is in service to collective learning. As a facilitator, you help the group maintain its focus on description and inquiry so the discussion is constructive and expansive rather than evaluative.

If you decide to hold students in the foreground of your observer's view and the teacher in the background, you will both decrease the teacher's vulnerability and mine the richest source for learning. With this foreground/background view, you can still see the teacher and what she is doing, yet more important, your eye is on the students' experience.

what they actually see and hear rather than interpretations and inferences. The T-chart (Fig. 11-5) has space on the page for questions, speculation, and thoughts.

With a discussion about new ideas and perspectives and an awareness of current research and professional literature, observers bring more knowledge and background to enrich what they are able to see.

TEXT DISCUSSION BEFORE OBSERVATION

This protocol (Fig. 11-4) works best when it is a short discussion that gets people's brains going, and enables you to hear from everyone. Looking for a passage to share gives purpose and provides a means of accountability for their reading.

This is ideal for groups of four to eight members. With a larger group, break into smaller groups for the discussion.

FIGURE 11-4: PROTOCOL

Text Discussion Prior to Observation

PURPOSE: New ideas to inform observation

MATERIALS: Common text

TIME: 20 minutes

STEPS

1. Choose a text that is relevant to the group's focus for the observation.

2. Each person selects a passage from the text that is significant to him or her and makes notes of his or her thinking about the passage.

3. Each person takes a turn reading his or her passage and explaining its personal meaning, including how it informs what we are working on in our classroom practice.

4. Each person has a chance to respond.

5. Steps 3 and 4 are repeated until everyone has had a chance to read a quote.

6. Notes are taken on essential ideas that the group has pulled from the text, especially those that might lead to specific next steps and action plans.

7. Debrief the process.

Tools for Leaders © 2007 Marjorie Larner, Scholastic Professional

---

DURING THE OBSERVATION: NOTE TAKING

During the observation, it is important that each person understand what is expected of him or her to contribute to the value and safety of the experience. A form serves as a scaffold to support constructive recording of observations.

Give the participants a double-column note-taking form (Fig. 11-5) to scaffold their observations and encourage them to record exactly what they see and hear separately from their own thinking and questions. Often, observers' ears and eyes are drawn to what stands out as needing attention; the tendency is to notice gaps and problems and make leaps to judge and interpret behaviors more than noticing exact words or actions.

In the form provided here, there is a space at the bottom to record ideas for practice that arise during the observation and/or during the discussion and debrief. This emphasizes the commitment to apply learning to improve classroom practice. Following is an example of a completed form (Fig. 11-6).

Even if someone doesn't want to use the form, its availability, as well as seeing it used by others in the group, will influence how observations are reported. Without notes to offer specific quotes and behaviors, the discussion wanders vaguely through impressions and thoughts. Therefore, while allowing choice for the form of note taking, do not make note taking itself optional. The discipline and accountability of note taking with a form helps guarantee a needed serious focus.

FIGURE 11-5: ORGANIZER

DOUBLE-ENTRY NOTE-TAKING FORM FOR OBSERVATION

Focus for observation:

Script what you see/hear	Record thoughts/questions

Implications for practice:

FIGURE 11-6

EXAMPLE OF DOUBLE-ENTRY NOTE-TAKING FORM

Focus for observation: *Implementing workshop model in language arts classroom*

Script what you see/hear	Record thoughts/questions
• Teacher modeled her own writing with a think-aloud of five attempts to get the lead she wanted • Offered instructional strategies to write goals in their notebooks • Status of the class/minute • Conferred to a number of kids in 15 minutes and then stayed with one for 15 minutes • Four main conferences and brief check-in interactions • Connected to past learning and imagined "rotten brussels sprouts" • Stayed in posted time frame • Student work shown all over classroom • Two boys asked: "What do you do?" • Kids talk to one another about their writing and their lead sentences • Kids found comfortable places of their choice to work • 2 minutes to get settled • Not all kids writing • One girl was crying about her writing and asked, "Will you help me?" • Kids talk with one another and with teacher about emotional and philosophical questions about life • ELL kids didn't say anything during discussion though their eyes were on whoever was speaking; one exception was _____ who made jokes	• Focus was simple; written on board, students fed off that • Tone of classroom: safety with emotions • Oral language is predominant • How many focus lessons have you done/do you plan to do on leads? • How will you assess the leads they do? • How can you make those kids who weren't writing get more focused? • How do you get different voices of expertise in the classroom? • How do you make sure they get the last 3 minutes to reflect on their own process and growth as writers? • What would happen if reflections were done as homework? • Lots of ways of having writers' voices in the room

Implications for practice:
• Connect past learning: show student work and thinking on walls
• Conferring in order to monitor every student's engagement
• Look at student work in small groups so different voices can be heard
• Modeling
• Talk to kids about being writers

AFTER THE OBSERVATION: DEBRIEF

After the observation, a little time to breathe and transition is usually necessary and appreciated. Give people time to get a drink, look over their notes, and chat about the experience. Then start with a structure for debriefing so the information will be conveyed efficiently and respectfully. Be clear about the purposes of the debrief, such as:

1. Observed teacher hears perspectives and information from varied points of view (literally varied points of view from different places around the room) for her own learning about her teaching, her students, and her classroom.

2. Observers and observed teacher share perspectives and explore implications for teaching, students, and classrooms.

In deciding how you will debrief, consider the amount of time you have and the primary purpose for the observation. Following are options (Fig. 11-7, 11-8, and 11-9) for structuring your debrief depending on the amount of time you have and the primary purpose of the observation.

GIVING AND RECEIVING FEEDBACK

The delicate nature of giving and receiving feedback cannot be stressed enough. The goal is that it be helpful and constructive. Feedback is most useful when it is given so that a person can hear it, believe it, and see implications for action. There is also a responsibility on the part of the person receiving feedback to listen with an open mind.

Take a few minutes to talk about negative and positive experiences (a nightmare and a helpful time) of giving and receiving feedback and what agreements and guidelines will be helpful.

Basic guidelines to keep in mind when giving feedback:

1. Give feedback related to the focus of the observation and be cautious about straying to other topics.

2. Be specific and concrete. Think of giving your colleague a picture of what you saw.

3. Listen to responses for further feedback that will be helpful.

> ### TROUBLESHOOTING: AVOIDING EVALUATIVE JUDGMENTS IN PEER OBSERVATIONS
>
> In the past, peer observations have often taken an evaluative form, which has worked powerfully for some and been disastrous for others. State clearly and explicitly that the one-on-one observation is more of an open-ended exploration and discovery process about instructional strategies than an evaluation of a teacher's use of instructional strategies.

FIGURE 11-7: PROTOCOL

Quick Debrief of Observation

PURPOSE: To provide feedback to teacher who was observed and to highlight key thoughts and questions raised through observation

TIME: 20–30 minutes

STEPS

1. Participants take a few minutes to read their notes from observation.
2. Conduct a group whip-around (go around the circle for each person to have a turn to speak or pass without pauses or discussion) focused on student learning and behaviors: What did you see and hear? Include instructional strategies and content when relevant to provide context. Each person offers one idea at a time. Continue whip-around until all ideas have been shared. Teacher listens and takes notes.
3. Conduct a group whip-around: Address questions this brings up for you.
4. Teacher responds with insights, questions, and observations.
5. The group brainstorms implications for teaching.
6. Debrief the process.

Tools for Leaders © 2007 Marjorie Larner, Scholastic Professional

FIGURE 11-8: PROTOCOL

Full Debrief of Observation

PURPOSE: To provide feedback to teacher who was observed and to explore key thoughts, questions, and implications that the group can generalize to other students and classrooms

TIME: 30–60 minutes

STEPS

1. Observers share what they saw and heard from students, in round-robin style, one comment at a time. Teacher listens and takes notes through Step 3.
2. Observers share what they saw and heard from teacher—instructional strategies and content.
3. Observers respond: What questions does this raise for you?
4. Teacher responds.
5. Whole group synthesizes:
   ◆ Essential learning and next steps to extend learning (for example, professional reading, discussion, observation)
   ◆ Implications for next steps to try in classrooms
6. Debrief the process: Was feedback given in a way that led to learning? What was comfortable? What was uncomfortable? What led to new thinking or a new view of teaching and learning? How might we improve this process?

Tools for Leaders © 2007 Marjorie Larner, Scholastic Professional

FIGURE 11-9: PROTOCOL

Debrief of Observation With a Large Group (12 or More)

PURPOSE: To include multiple perspectives and insights in an efficient debrief of observation of teacher who was observed; to explore key thoughts, questions, and implications that can be generalized to other students and classrooms

TIME: 45 minutes

STEPS

1. Start in groups of three to five. If you have identified essential questions, each group might select one question as a focus for their debrief.

2. Share what you saw. Discuss instructional implications.

3. Determine what you will share with the larger group; include summary of what you saw, instructional implications, recommended next steps, or topics for further discussion/observation.

4. Reconvene the whole group.

5. Request a report of essential learning from each smaller group.

6. Discuss common basic principles of effective teaching and learning, implications, and next steps.

7. Debrief the process.

FIGURE 11-10: PROTOCOL

Variation: One-on-One Observations

PURPOSE: To provide an opportunity for two teachers or a teacher and a coach to engage in observations for focused learning and mutual support without complicated logistical arrangements or the high level of risk that sometimes accompanies larger observation groups

This format can work well for a coach with an individual teacher, or the coach can support partners to do this on their own, which will build capacity for teachers coaching each other.

Coaches can also help observation partners:

◆ Facilitate their debrief session.

◆ Build in time with a larger group, to do an extended debrief.

◆ Help them figure out logistical arrangements for classroom coverage.

◆ Cover one of the classrooms to release the teacher for observing.

STEPS

1. **Identify focus and purpose:** Two teachers, often part of a larger group with a common purpose, identify a shared focus or question. This may also include a common reading or instructional strategy they are both learning to apply in their classrooms.

2. **Arrange schedule and time:** There are different arrangements they can make in order to observe and share feedback, from fitting it into planning times, lunch, and after school, to creative coverage of classes by non-classroom school staff to subs releasing them for a half or full day (sub steps aside for classroom teacher to be observed). With a half or full day to spend together observing and debriefing, teachers will have an opportunity to go deeper in exploring implications and applications.

3. **Document and record:** Share the observation notes with the observed teacher to reflect on in her own time.

4. **Articulate new learning:** Share new insights, validation, and surprises and discuss what you will do differently in your classrooms. Teachers have learned that it helps if they record these insights so they can refer back to them. This will also serve as a useful document for reporting to sponsors if further funding support is requested.

5. **Extend:** Meet with larger group or whole faculty to share experience, insights, reflections.

6. **Follow-up:** Set a time on your calendars to meet and talk about new practice as a result of the observation and discussion. Share new insights and questions.

Tools for Leaders © 2007 Marjorie Larner, Scholastic Professional

Keep these guidelines in mind when receiving feedback:

1. Be specific about a focus for the observation and what kind of feedback you would like.

2. Breathe and listen without forming judgments. Take notes as you listen if that will help you sort out what you are hearing.

3. Summarize and synthesize, clarify what you hear, and ask for specific examples.

SCHOOL WALK

There is so much to see in every inch of a school building. I notice that I have habits that draw my eyes to certain parts of the hallways and classrooms. When we take a focused walk through a building, I notice things I never saw before or I see them from a new perspective.

PRINCIPLE

The School Walk protocol (Fig. 11-11) was originally developed as a means for school visitors to have a meaningful interchange with hosting educators about their observations of the school. It is also useful when resident teachers visit areas of their school they don't generally visit, or see familiar areas with new eyes, so they see the grander context in which their classrooms reside.

CONSIDERATIONS

With an observer's point of view, you will see hallways and lunchrooms with a new perspective. It is a chance for colleagues to see one another's classrooms, develop a big picture of your school community, and gain insight into what children experience. This is an excellent process in which to include parents and other non-teaching members of the school community.

FIGURE 11-11: ACTIVITY

School Walk

TIME: 45–60 minutes

STEPS (Read through steps before you begin.)

The protocol can be used while school is in session or after school hours, depending on whether your purpose requires that students be in the building.

1. **Identify Focus or Question:** It may be an open-ended walk-through, or you may have a particular question in terms of school climate, student engagement, differentiation opportunities, and so on.

2. **Offer directions and hints for the walk:**
   - Look at your school and participate in the protocol with a beginner's mind.
   - Understand this is a quick walk-through to see what is on the surface—what is visible and stands out—like a snapshot of a moment in time.
   - Designate a timekeeper to keep people from stopping too long in one place.
   - Take notes as you walk through.

3. **Walk through:** Walk through the school for 20–30 minutes. Make nonevaluative observations, avoiding qualitative judgments about what you see. As you walk, consider the following questions:
   - What do you see? What don't you see?
   - What do you wonder about?
   - What do you think this school is working on?

4. **Share observations:** Return to the large group and share your findings on the questions in sequence.

5. **Reflect:** Reflect aloud on what surprised and interested you and what you saw during the walk that was new.

6. **Synthesize:** Discuss what you heard in terms of themes, commonalities, and differences while traversing the building; address steps to take to support your school goals or the particular goals you're focusing on for the school walk.

7. **Debrief:** Was this protocol valuable? How could it have been better? How might this protocol be put to use in the future?

Adapted by Edorah Frazier from the Collaborative Conference, originally developed by Steve Seidel

Tools for Leaders © 2007 Marjorie Larner, Scholastic Professional

Field Notes

We used our classrooms, our students and ourselves as the resources for this study.
— teacher reflection

At Aspen Creek K–8 in Broomfield, Colorado, whenever a question or challenge arises, Principal Scott Winston's response is "Let's put together a lab to study this issue." He then puts out an invitation to all the teachers for volunteers to join the study, usually for two to four meetings. He uses funds provided by the PTA and the district to pay for release time for teachers and usually some good refreshments. A coach, or teacher leader, facilitates the discussions and other tasks are usually divided among participants. In past years, they have focused on school climate, the research process, boys and literacy, essential questions about best practice . . . the list goes on.

With each lab, the school has refined and developed its process and methods. These labs follow a standard format that allows for ever evolving variations, which the teachers develop to meet the needs of that particular study. Observations are always the center-piece of their plans, along with readings, surveys, and interviews, and sharing their learning, questions, and recommendations with the entire faculty for discussion and further recommendations.

CHAPTER 12
FROM A STUDENT'S
PERSPECTIVE

We have ended the silence that keeps us apart.
— Margaret Wheatley

We talk about "students at the center." We think about them all the time. We make educated guesses about what they need and how to provide it. Yet it is not often that we have an opportunity to stop and listen to what our students can tell us about what they are experiencing.

Part of my job often includes sitting one-on-one with students to find out what they are thinking, what is helping them or making school life harder for them. I always learn something, whether it is about that individual student, the school, or a transferable insight about students in general. I am always amazed by teenagers' willingness to open up to a near stranger who shows interest and by the ability of even the youngest primary students to provide profound insights on school life and learning.

If you start looking, you can find numerous ways to learn more about what students experience and see in your school. You might be surprised, or your perceptions might be validated. You are likely to learn something new that will expand your perspective on what you can do as a teacher and, as a bonus, make a connection to a great young person.

AIM: HEARING DIRECTLY FROM STUDENTS

Since students are the reason our schools even exist, it makes sense to me to find out what they are seeing, thinking, and experiencing. With one-on-one or small-group conversations, students usually seem honored and eager to have a receptive, interested audience for their opinions and thoughts.

CONSIDERATIONS

Some of my best conversations with kids of any age or gender or cultural background happened as we were walking down the hall or working on a project together, especially while fixing something that had broken. Those spontaneous, great discussions certainly have value.

But when you have a specific purpose, it is helpful to carefully plan the questions to ask, the way you approach particular students, the setting, and the timing. (See Fig. 12-1.) The formality of an interview conveys a seriousness and importance about hearing what they have to say, and they almost always respond with matching seriousness.

> ### To Teachers
>
> I like to imagine I am getting a glimpse of the school through students' eyes. We have actually given students video cameras to walk around the school videotaping what catches their eye. Each student gets five minutes to tape, so they are thoughtful about what they want to show. When we watch, we truly get a glimpse through their eyes of what stands out in the school.

GUIDELINES

- One-on-one or small-group interview/conversations are a good place to start. This can be a positive experience for kids when they do not feel grilled but rather invited to speak their minds.
- Younger children often do best in short conversations that are folded into their day rather than when they're pulled out, especially with an adult they don't know well.
- Teachers usually know which of their students would feel less pressure as part of a group and those who would be more open on their own.
- If you ask one question right after the other, they may feel as if they are being grilled. Try to make it conversational. Offer brief positive responses and your own thoughts in between asking questions.
- Some people speculate that boys generally aren't comfortable in face-to-face close contact, so you might want to consider sitting side by side.

FIGURE 12-1: PROTOCOL

Interview Steps

PURPOSE: Careful planning before talking with a student to identify outcomes

STEPS

1. Frame a guiding question that is based on what you want to learn from the interview.

2. Frame interview questions. In the context of talking with a student, each person will probably use his or her own words, but it is helpful to have a common base to start.

3. Create a T-chart (see Fig. 11-5) with the questions to organize your note taking.

4. When you start talking with the student: (a) explain your purpose for asking him or her questions; (b) ask the student for permission to take notes so you can remember exact words. If you don't feel comfortable taking notes during the interview, make sure you jot some notes immediately afterward, before you start to forget.

5. Reconvene as a whole group. Using the questions you had identified, share what students said, especially direct quotes.

6. Look for patterns, themes, questions raised.

7. Identify next steps (e.g., gather more information, share data with colleagues, change practice).

8. Debrief the process. Did you get the information you had hoped for? How was it talking with the kids? Did they seem open and forthcoming?

Tools for Leaders © 2007 Marjorie Larner, Scholastic Professional

AIM: FOCUSING ON INDIVIDUAL STUDENTS

Questions and thoughts about problems with students often dominate teachers' attention as well as their conversations. However, that informal "kid talk" is not always productive. If the talk doesn't resolve the problem, it may in fact further aggravate it. I have heard teachers say how frustrated they were listening to complaints and problems with no hope of moving out of the dilemma. If you bring structure to the conversation, with a focus on finding new perspectives and ideas, you can achieve a more satisfying result.

CONSIDERATIONS

A simple structure such as Brief Responses to Challenges (Fig. 9-7) will organize the discussion to be productive and brief without making people feel too controlled. If you want to go further, you could use a consultancy protocol (Fig. 9-4 or 9-5).

Many years ago Patricia Carini and teachers at the Prospect School in Vermont began to look in depth at one child from multiple perspectives, and their method remains one of the most important tools for my learning. Since I believe this process requires skillful, experienced facilitation, it is beyond the scope of this book to adequately present it as a viable tool. If you are interested in learning more about this process, you can find a version on the National School Reform Faculty Web site (www.nsrfharmony.org); for more on the original version, I highly recommend *From Another Angle: Children's Strengths and School Standards* by Margaret Himley with Patricia Carini (2000). (See References for more information on both these resources.)

You can also shift the conversation about students toward learning by using information that comes directly from them through their work.

AIM: LEARNING FROM STUDENT WORK

Student work is a very powerful primary resource for information about students' learning and their responses to our instruction. Most of the time, student work is the ultimate evidence of what students are doing, what they are able to do, and how they meet expectations communicated in the classroom. The work can provide clues as to how students approach a task, how they are hearing expectations, where their attention is focused, and so on. Along with classroom observations and data analysis, student work is a vital component of a full picture of a teacher's task.

When teachers have a question or dilemma about their teaching and learning or a particular student, ask them to consider presenting student work to colleagues, using a protocol for a systematic and constructive process to shed light on the question. As a facilitator, you support the teacher who is presenting to frame the question, to choose student work, and to choose a protocol or process that will lead the group to provide helpful feedback.

There are many structures and guidelines you can use to ensure that the experience is productive for all concerned, especially for a teacher who presents student work from her classroom. Tight structures with an unvarying format ensure quality discussion, superseding ingrained habits of evaluating for deficits and gaps, and are often used to achieve results in a short time frame and to maintain respect for teacher and student.

At the end of each meeting where you have looked at student work, just as with observing or walking through the school, it is vital to debrief the process with particular attention to how the presenting teacher felt and what she takes with her. And then, allow each person an opportunity to share what he or she has learned to take back to the classroom.

CONSIDERATIONS

In my experience, there are many pitfalls to facilitating a group of teachers looking at student work. Foremost among the challenges is ensuring that the purpose is not to evaluate or focus on gaps, which is the more traditional task for teachers. Seeing what is there rather than what is not there requires a big shift in perspective and a suspension of our usual judgment. It usually takes practice, but the benefits of close, nonjudgmental observation of student work far exceed the challenges. The goal is to give the student the benefit of the doubt and to understand that beyond the level of skill reflected in the student's work is a desire to succeed. The two protocols that follow (Fig. 12-2 and 12-3) present minimal personal risk for individual teachers, so they are a good place to start.

FIGURE 12-2: PROTOCOL

Looking at Patterns in Student Work

This is a good introductory protocol for looking at student work, as it does not focus on performance of one student or one teacher and instead focuses on inquiry into a group question through a range of work from students in multiple classrooms.

PURPOSE: By examining patterns, themes, and inconsistencies, you gain insight about a particular population or large group of students and are able to draw conclusions and generate implications for instruction in general, without targeting any one teacher.

TIME: 45 minutes

STEPS:

1. Bring samples of student work that represent the population or question you want to address—they can be random, or they can be chosen to present a range or demonstrate particular points in student performance.

2. Pass the work around the circle. Look for patterns, contradictions, and themes. It is helpful to take notes.

3. Discuss patterns, contradictions, and themes.

4. Share questions that these patterns and themes raise for you; discuss implications for further study.

5. Establish next steps.

FOLLOW-UP: One teacher brings work from an individual student that relates to the questions and implications raised. This might be student work that represents a breakthrough, a struggle, or a range of performance.

Tools for Leaders © 2007 Marjorie Larner, Scholastic Professional

---

FIGURE 12-3: PROTOCOL

Modified Consultancy for Examining Student Work

PURPOSE: Bring in other perspectives to think more expansively about a particular question regarding a student with a focus on his or her work to inform the discussion.

TIME: 45–60 minutes

STEPS (Read the steps before you begin.)

1. The presenter offers a context for the student work. (5 minutes)
   - Assignment or expectations
   - Conditions under which the work was done
   - Any other relevant descriptions
   - Framing question

2. The group examines the student work. (5 minutes)

3. Each person describes one aspect of the work—comments are purely descriptive, not evaluative (e.g., "The student uses dialogue marked by quotation marks," as opposed to "The student knows how to use quotation marks"). (5 minutes)

4. The presenter listens and takes notes. (This is so the presenter can see the work through others' eyes.)

5. The group asks clarifying questions. (5 minutes)

6. The group asks probing questions of the presenter. The presenter writes the questions as they are asked but does not respond. (7 minutes)

7. The presenter responds aloud to those questions she deems helpful and probing. (5 minutes)

8. The presenter once again moves outside of the group to listen as participants discuss the student work, in light of the questions framed for the group by the presenter.

9. **Option:** Some groups like to begin the conversation with warm feedback—strengths in the presentation or in the student's work in relation to the presenting teacher's questions, followed by cooler feedback, such as questions raised and gaps in the work or in what the presenter has considered. Sometimes the group will raise questions for the presenter to consider ("I wonder what would happen if . . ." or "I wonder why . . ."). The presenter listens and takes notes, but does not participate in this discussion. (15 minutes)

10. The presenter responds to what she or he has heard. (5–10 minutes)

11. A whole-group discussion can then take place if time allows. (5–10 minutes)

12. Debrief the process, with particular attention to the comfort level and benefit of the process for the presenter. (5 minutes)

Developed in the field by educators affiliated with the NSRF

Tools for Leaders © 2007 Marjorie Larner, Scholastic Professional

AIM: USING DATA

The only real mistake is one from which we learn nothing.
— John Powell

There are many programs and approaches to help you analyze data to inform your instruction. I think the most useful include multiple types of data and simple structures connected to the reality of your classrooms that support your conversation and thinking.

CONSIDERATIONS

Your clearly established intention and/or goal is your filter to analyze and synthesize information. For instance, if your group is meeting to determine why there aren't more students representing minority populations in advanced classes, you would look at the data differently than if you were focused on the number of students scoring 4 or higher on AP exams. With the first focus you might ask where students are instead of in advanced-level classes. With the latter focus, you might look at how they prepare for the exam. (See Fig. 12-4 and 12-5.)

EXAMPLE OF DATA PUT TO USE

Middle and high school Spanish teachers met to consider why so many students didn't succeed in the transition from Spanish I to Spanish II. Figure 12-5 shows how they organized their data and put it to use.

FIGURE 12-4

EXAMPLE DATA ANALYSIS ORGANIZER

INTENDED OUTCOME OF ANALYSIS:

Summary of Quantifiable Data (e.g., test scores, grade-point averages, attendance records, referrals (disciplinary, academic), enrollment patterns, graduation rates)

Grade averages from Spanish I to Spanish II (including those for students in middle school as well as those making transition to high school

Enrollment patterns (who drops out and when dropouts occur)

Summary of Qualitative Data (e.g., observations, interviews, surveys, questionnaires, teacher records, anecdotal records)

Teacher anecdotal observations: characteristics of students who are successful in Spanish II
Student end-of-year surveys

Patterns

Even when Spanish II was taken at the middle school level, there was a high failure rate.

Contradictions

Some students continue taking Spanish through all their years in high school.

Themes and Threads

Students and teachers identify struggles with Spanish II.

Inferences Supported by Several Kinds of Data

Problem lies in transition from Spanish I to Spanish II or in the Spanish II curriculum, exacerbated when it coincided with the transition to high school.

FIGURE 12-4, PAGE 2

Surprises and Inferences Not Supported by Data
It is possible that it is not just that students are not trying.
There is a wide variation in each teacher's approach and yet some similarity in the struggles students experience.

Other Data That Would Be Useful
Compare grades that students get in these Spanish classes with GPA or grades in other courses, particularly language arts.
Check attendance patterns.
Collect data from other schools regarding Spanish II success for students.

Questions
Do other schools see the same challenges?
What are current views on most effective approach to teaching world languages?
How can teachers work together to come to consensus about the issues and the solutions?

Implications and Recommendations for Action
Discuss different philosophies and strategies for foreign-language acquisition. What does research say?
Look at entire curriculum and the implications for sequence, course options.
Support from district to find consensus on philosophical, strategic approach to language acquisition in the district.
Consider new course options that would support success for a wider range of students.
Make a connection with a tutoring center at a school to be part of getting to students who need individual help.

Commitments: Plan and Timeline
Plan is to gather more information to guide change in curriculum and course options, perhaps in instructional approaches.
Talk with teachers from schools who have made curriculum and instructional changes (each person identified one other teacher to contact in next month).
Observe and interview students who represent range of success in our curriculum as it is (we will each talk with two students from our classes).
We want a commitment from everyone to make changes to address this ongoing challenge, so we will arrange a meeting with everyone who has a part in a plan to make changes in curriculum (district, teachers, department heads, school administrators). We will report our data, make recommendations, ask for discussion, and plan at that point.

Follow-Up
We will be meeting to do the above.
Identify a date by which we want to have a new plan in place for the following year.

Debriefing Process
Would have been helpful to have every teacher of world languages at this meeting. We were able to be open and honest and find options for next steps.

FIGURE 12-5: ORGANIZER

DATA ANALYSIS

INTENDED OUTCOME OF ANALYSIS:
Summary of Quantifiable Data (e.g., test scores, grade-point averages, attendance records, referrals (disciplinary, academic), enrollment patterns, graduation rates)
Summary of Qualitative Data (e.g., observations, interviews, surveys, questionnaires, teacher records, anecdotal records)
Patterns
Contradictions
Themes and Threads
Inferences Supported by Several Kinds of Data

FIGURE 12-5, PAGE 2

Surprises and Inferences Not Supported by Data

Other Data That Would Be Useful

Questions

Implications and Recommendations for Action

Commitments: Plan and Timeline

Follow-Up

Debriefing Process

FIELD NOTES

The question about boys not getting what they need in school became a hot topic for many schools in recent years, with many opinions and questions raised. In a K–8 school, teachers met to look at this issue with the intention of discovering how to provide more effectively for boys.

They looked at boys' writing samples, test scores, and grades; interviewed students; and brought in their own observations and personal experience. They read books and articles and found multiple perspectives from results in different studies. They shared their assumptions, concerns, and hunches about what was going on.

The group identified three questions that kept coming up:

◆ What motivates and engages boys in learning and performing, particularly in reading and writing?

◆ Should we cater to their interests in sports, conflict, and media?

◆ What prevents boys from meeting standards for proficiency in reading and writing?

After bringing their questions to the whole faculty for further discussion, the teachers narrowed the three questions down to one. They wanted to test out their hunch about the impact of freedom and choice on motivation and engagement. They decided this was a question to test out with both boys and girls. They formulated an action research plan.

FIGURE 12-6: PROTOCOL

Conducting Teacher Inquiry and Research

PURPOSE: With complex questions around tough issues that have significant impact in the school, it is useful to use a systematic process to explore and analyze possible interventions.

STEPS

1. Frame the question.

2. Gather baseline information (data, student interviews, observations, discussions).

3. Identify an instructional intervention related to the question.

4. Devise a plan for collecting post-intervention information (scores, observations, surveys, interviews).

5. Compare and contrast baseline and post-intervention data. You could use the Data Analysis organizer (Fig. 12-5) for this step.

6. Discuss implications and next steps.

Tools for Leaders © 2007 Marjorie Larner, Scholastic Professional

---

This is not scientifically pure research because there is no plan to control variables with a control group. However, this is a valid model for qualitative research. Perhaps more significantly, the project brought together a whole school to see what they could discover about reaching reluctant readers and writers through one small but consistent intervention.

Question: If boys are given freedom to write about what matters to them and what is personally fascinating, will they engage more enthusiastically and prolifically in the act and study of writing?

Steps:

1. An invitation was issued to every teacher (including those teaching electives) to commit to providing 15 minutes of free journaling time at least once every week through at least the first semester. The response was surprisingly unanimous for participation.

2. Explicit guidelines for the intervention were developed by teachers, based on a successful model followed by first-grade teachers.

3. Baseline, midyear and end-of-year data collected included the following:
   - Interview sample of students with a set of questions
   - Teacher surveys on boys' engagement and performance
   - Grades
   - Standardized test results
   - Writing samples scored by a group of teachers

This project was a focal point for discussion among teachers at all grade levels, as they now had a common practice that everyone was not only using but using with a meta-cognitive eye toward how it worked for students. The precedent was set for questioning current practice as a whole faculty and working together to investigate potential instructional improvements. Because it emerged from teacher conversations and their collective ideas and questions, the impact of this one small intervention was actually much bigger than they had realized, with many unintended and positive consequences for the whole school community.

AFTERWORD

Think about how amazing teaching could be if we all had the ability to truly step back, reflect, take a deep breath, take risks, change and then . . . dive in!
— teacher reflection

At the end of a Bollywood movie, when the lovers are finally united and harmony is restored to the community, I always feel a little tension because I just know this moment of stillness is not going to last. Drama will find them again. I want to stay and watch: what unfolds next?

I also find it hard to leave a building after a meeting or a workshop. I want to offer just one more encouraging story or idea that will make everything smooth and guarantee success. One more tool that will save the participants on a hard day. One last question to shift perspective.

What is a good way to end? I don't always catch myself before uttering what Jeff Wein calls the consultant's famous last words, "Good-bye and good luck," which I used to perceive as a cynical statement. Now I see there is actually a wonderful truth underlying these words. Coaching and instructional leadership are not actually about me, or any one person, but are tools and opportunities that can be passed on to help teachers fulfill their goals and dreams for their students.

When Maya Angelou was asked, on her 70th birthday, what she had learned in her life, she concluded a fairly long list with "I've learned that people will forget what you said, people will forget what you did, but people will never forget how you made them feel."

Perhaps that is the message to carry with you. As a leader, you have the chance to support your school community working and learning together with an increased sense of joy and efficacy and making a difference for every student.

In the end, I leave carrying stories of children and adults with whom I have worked. Patricia Carini says stories "feed the spirit and spark imagination, inspire dreams of the future." I began this book with a story of a boy I cannot forget, who had been let down by our system repeatedly (see Introduction). His teacher and I pushed for a group to help her think about how to resolve the dilemma. When they listened to her stories of the contrast in his behavior with just one intervention, they devised a plan in which different people could commit to that 20-minute period on different days. Over time, he was not as dependent on getting a full 20 minutes of attention. But he still needed the arrangement under times of stress, such as before vacations or at test time. He established relationships with many adults in the building, increasing his social capacity and flexibility and giving him a sense of community support and belonging. We began to hope that he might have the resiliency needed to pull himself out of the situation into which he had been born.

We found our intervention not only helped *him*, but also the staff. For with the celebration that grew from the extra time the staff made for him, they began to look for ways to share responsibility for other students with overwhelming needs.

The story that can unfold in your school will probably be different from this one. Your characters and setting are unique. Yet the tension is similar for us all: to meet the needs of different children with a range of issues and capacities; to provide equal access regardless of background or class; to motivate, inspire, and engage; and to teach, within a community of learners. Sometimes, as my friend Carrie Symons says, the solutions are simple. Usually, it takes all of us.

References

Allen, D., & Blythe, T. (2004). *The facilitator's book of questions: Tools for looking together at student and teacher work.* New York: Teachers College Press.

Ambrose, D. (1987). *Managing complex change.* Pittsburgh, PA: The Enterprise Group.

Anderson, C. (2000). *How's it going? A practical guide to conferring with student writers.* Portsmouth, NH: Heinemann.

Atwell, N. (2007). *The reading zone.* New York: Scholastic.

Blythe, T., Allen, D., & Powell, B.S. (1999). *Looking together at student work: A companion guide to assessing student learning.* New York: Teachers College Press.

Carini, P. (2001). *Starting strong: A different look at children, schools, and standards.* New York: Teachers College Press.

Cisneros, S. (1992). *Woman Hollering Creek and other stories.* New York: Vintage Contemporaries.

Esch, T., & Stefano, G. B. (2004). The neurobiology of pleasure, reward processes, addiction and their health implications. *Neuroendocrinology Letters, 25*(4), 235–51.

Franklin, B. (1987). Remarks concerning the savages of North America. In J. A. Lemay (Ed.), *Franklin: Writings.* New York: The Library of America.

Fullan, M. (1999). *Change forces: The sequel.* London: Falmer Press.

GaWaNi Pony Boy. (1998). *Horse, follow closely.* Irvine, CA: Bow Tie Press.

Harvey, S., & Goudvis, A. (2005). *The comprehension toolkit: Language and lessons for active literacy.* Portsmouth, NH: Heinemann.

Himley, M., & Carini, P. (Eds.). (2000). *From another angle: Children's strengths and school standards.* New York: Teachers College Press.

Houston, J., with Rubin, M. (1995). *Manual for the peacemaker: An Iroquois legend to heal self and society.* Wheaton, IL: Quest Books.

Hughes, L. (2002). Simple speaks his mind. In D. S. Harper (Ed.), *The early Simple stories.* Columbia, MO: University of Missouri Press

Killion, J. P., & Simmons, L. A. (1992). The Zen of facilitation. *Journal of Staff Development, 13*(3), 127–130.

Johnston, P. H. (2004). *Choice words: How our language affects children's learning.* Portland, ME: Stenhouse.

Leinberger, P., & Tucker, B. (1991). *The new individualists: The generation after the organization man.* New York: HarperCollins.

McDonald, J. P., Mohr, N., Dichter, A., & McDonald, E. C. (2003). *The power of protocols: An educator's guide to better practice.* New York: Teachers College Press.

Partnership for 21st Century Skills. (2006). *Results that matter: 21st century skills and high school reform.* (2006). Retrieved October 23, 2006 from http://www.21stcenturyskills.org/documents/RTM2006.pdf

Pearson, P. D., Dole, J. A., Duffy, G. G., & Roehler, L. R. (1992). Developing expertise in reading comprehension: What should be taught and how should it be taught? In A. Farstrup and S. J. Samuels (Eds.), *What research has to say about reading instruction* (2nd ed.). Newark, DE: International Reading Association.

Ritchhart, R. (2002). *Intellectual character: What it is, why it matters, and how to get it.* San Francisco: Jossey-Bass.

Stevens, W. D., with Kahne, J. E. (2006). *Professional communities and instructional improvement practices: A study of small high schools in Chicago.* Retrieved October 23, 2006, from University of Chicago, Consortium on Chicago School Research web site http://ccsr.uchicago.edu/content/publications.php?pub_id=8

Taylor-Hall, M. A. (1995). *Come and go, Molly Snow.* New York: W. W. Norton.

Walker, B. (1997). Understanding the diversity teaching terrain. In J. V. Gallos and V. J. Ramsey (Eds.), *Teaching diversity: Listening to the soul, speaking from the heart.* San Francisco: Jossey-Bass.

Weissglass, J. (1997). Deepening our dialogue about equity. *Educational Leadership, 54*(7), 78–81.

Wheatley, M. J. (2002). *Turning to one another: Simple conversations to restore hope to the future.* San Francisco: Berrett-Koehler Publishers.

Wiggins, G., & McTighe, J. (2006). Examining the teaching life. *Educational Leadership, 63*(6), 26–29.

Wilhelm, J. (2002). *Action strategies for deepening comprehension.* New York: Scholastic

Zemelman, S., & Daniels, H. (2004). *Subjects matter: Every teacher's guide to content-area reading.* Portsmouth, NH: Heinemann.

RECOMMENDED WEB SITES AND RESOURCES

National Center for Research on Evaluation, Standards, and Student Testing (CRESST): http://www.cse.ucla.edu

Tools for School-Improvement Planning (Annenberg Institute for School Reform): http://www.annenberginstitute.org/tools/

National School Reform Faculty (NSRF): http://www.harmonyschool.org/nsrf/

Colorado Critical Friends Group (CCFG): http://www.coloradocfg.org

Prospect Center for Education and Research: http://www.prospectcenter.org

Lesson Study Research Group: http://www.tc.columbia.edu/lessonstudy/lessonstudy.html

INDEX